Holding the World Up

© Copyright 2020 Robert Cole

One Hundred Twenty-Four
Short Stories

Robert Cole

Contact Falcons Press

falconspress.com

info@falconspress.com

**WGAW Registered
2081003**

Falcons Press

Box 4073, Medford, OR 97501

Falcons Press ◇ com
≈ Publishers of Wonderful Things

info@falconspress.com

ISBN-13:978-1-7336257-2-2

Library of Congress Control Number: 2020920244

Produced in the United States of America

①

Contents

Bathroom

I was just in the shower, mumbling to myself, when a young (inexperienced) long-leg spider attacked from the high corner.

All pissed off about the wet. He'd had it.

I pulled him by his thread to the shampoo bottles, but he rushed me on the tub lip. I rebuffed him by tapping the wall.

Instantaneous charges followed forced retreats.

Finally I loomed over him, allowing the full weight of my overbearing human form to sink in.

- I got out with the towel.

He's still commanding the shampoo, AND HE THINKS HE WON!

> (... He wouldn't even know about the shampoo
> if it weren't for me.)

The Frog

It was raining. A storm of many days poured, the first storm of the season.

Raymond had definite philosophy. Held within definite perimeters, Raymond was all knowing.

By self proclamation, Raymond was King. Raymond held court.

King Raymond.

Raymond, with his changing entourage, was ensconced at my house; and like the rain, would be for the season.

This night Raymond would be tested.

It was a long drive from "over-the-hill."

Twilight gave way to night. The rain came in sheets as the headlights flashed back and forth across the turning country road.

We huddle in our cocoon, oblivious to the cow pastures passing us in the dark.

Leaping from the pavement, the splashing water is like little lightning bolts. Some are frogs. You know some are frogs because you can see them now and then. We gently careen to miss as many as possible.

In a creative perk, Tui's old man pulls over and jumps from the car. His figure flashes in the headlamp's glare like the rain. Disappearing and returning in the light, he darts through the sheeting downpour.

He has grabbed one of those little jumping frogs.

The little jumping frog turns out to have a body about 3" x 4". Long legs dangle. What girth!

Our large friend is attired in a "Camo" style skin pattern displaying huge red spots. He seems less enamored with us than we with him, being distinctly indifferent to this new scene thrust before him.

Tui pops him into a small paper bag, and we proceed down this back coastal highway to our town.

We bump up on "the Mesa", a plateau-like rise which provides most of the residential property for the area, and come before the house. This is the house of "King Raymond, the All Knowing." This is my house but now it's King Raymond's.

We three spring hopscotch through the puddles to the door.

Our fresh spirit is not dampened by the enveloping warmth. Bright light and good cheer fill the home.

Raymond is in the bedroom, in good form and holding court.

The test of King Raymond flows without plan.

Tui holds the bag up before his majesty and begs, "Bet you can't guess what's in here!"

Without the slightest hesitation nor hint of care he returns, "A big red-spotted frog."

Raymond is King.

The Fly

It was 10:40 in the morning when that bugger started cruising breakfast. He had a wondrous space for his runs. Pre-Victorian. Twenty foot ceilings. Lush green at play out the overly tall kitchen window.

Did he want our breakfast or the patches of sun igniting the table?

Great comfort promised to bribe my past annoyances when he landed in the sink. A flip of the tap ...and down he goes!

When retrieving the plates, I heard it. Over there, - in the sink. Was it a buzz?

Peering down, the dark grid sat empty at first. Then out of the brass poked his little head.

By the time I got my hand to the spigot, he was up on the drain flitting the water from his only hampered wing.

"Too late, buddy!"

Really blasted him. The little black dot flushed high up and around the large basin on a huge tidal. I had to wait while it drained.

There he went. Follow with huge blast. I watch it drain. He's GONE.

Back to the paper. Bright sun streaming on page three.

...What's that sound? A trumpeting from far off?

I stare forward; he's buzzing down in that tube.

Hot water this time. NO SYMPATHY!

"GONE - SUCKER!"

With a feeling of great rectitude, I strode from the counter. The master of the castle. The righter of wrongs. And, to doting spousal approval, I have healed the morning solitude.

Page four. I read, - listening.

I glance over... she's staring across her coffee, - listening.

I start to re-read. -Woop! There he is.

We leap to the sink. With a half buzz, he pops over the brass lip.

Hot coffee. Hot water. Hot soup. Old spaghetti! - mashed down.

More hot water. - We watch it drain.
She empties the coffee pot. - We watch it drain
More hot water. - We watch it drain.

Ahhh. Page five.

It suddenly occurs to us a certain melancholy pervades. It's only natural after such battle. Still, he stood it like no other. What other fly could have survived even the first blast?

No other fly. - I feel kind'a bad.

She's up at the sink, looking down. The steam is settling on the window; the spider plant drips no more.

I go to the sink with her, two mourners at the wake.

The soap dish allows another drip.

When that drop hits the porcelain, an odd ring catches the air...

Her pupils meet mine. "IT'S HIM!!!"

Will he make it? He must be under the house, below the first story.

We wait, listening to the slow, faint echoes spiraling up the drain. What labors. It must be slimy in those pipes; how does he do it?

Will he do it? He must be utterly exhausted. - I'm utterly exhausted!

Suddenly it's closer. We look at each other, then at the drain. Squinting to see something move in the grid. Finally, he pokes up. With effort, he pulls onto the lip.

He's limp, exhausted. Totally soaked. - Looks like a dead fly.

Spouse looks disappointed. We're both sad.

How can this fly be dead? It just made it up the drain pipe from hell! It came through the worst punishment of the modern world.

It crawled up from the bowels of this building (I have a hard time with the stairs).

I run to the bathroom and grab a roll of tissue. Ripping little shards of paper, I wick his inundated body. He doesn't look good! I surgically daub our friend's privates. Half inch strips are soaked and tossed.

I rest him in a bed of tissue on the warm sill. I gently blow trying to dry him. You can't see his wings, they're still too wet laying up against his body. Is he alive?

I blow until his wings start to fluff.

He doesn't move.

We stop and look at him. He doesn't move.

We get very close and look right at him. Motionless.

Then quietly, he picks his head up and flicks us a buzz.

About twenty minutes pass before, with appropriate fanfare and much adulation, we release him from the back porch.

_____

Although many years, I still see him now and then; when he comes around.
But I don't let him in.

Marsha

Jim pointed her out. I hadn't noticed her before. Not in any "special way." Not like now.

She was small, dark skinned; a certain gold or red inference in her long, deep tawny brown hair. She had full lips and doe eyes.

She was beautiful.

A mysterious beauty.

She had an energy. She seemed to have one or two closer friends, but all the girls swirled about her.

All under her direction. And all happy to be so. Even the very most beautiful and most popular. All excited by her lead.

She was at the center. The controlling energy. Not at the top, strangely.

Somehow she seemed a loner. More actually, alone.

Alone by group acceptance. Love by common decree, no jealousy.

It had been several days since Jim's affections for her had been confessed, and nothing could interrupt the constant dance of her vision in my thoughts.

It was Wednesday morning. Ten O'clock.

I bolted from conversation and galloped in a wide arc

through the thirty or so admiring females in joyous or-chestration to the center. My hands slapping my trousers like holsters.

Skipping up, slappity-slap, I kissed her warm cheek; and galloped off.

I was eight.

Takahashi

The void. Used or held. A world. Or a point.

The void of the Five Elements, Earth, Water, Wind,
Fire, Void.

Void was the aether of the Greeks; and of Europe. It
is the Black Hole.
It is the pull of things not.

The void was in the crevice of the swordsman's
palm. That place between the Five Thousand Places of
the hand. That malleable cleft between the Five, each
of a thousand, lubricated with the Void. A place of no
place.

"The Void will swallow your opponent. Swallow him
up."

- The words of Sensei

The void is also in the end of the sword pommel, the
"KASHIRA." What was the butt of the sword handle is
now a ring, - opening a hole to the end of the world.

"It will suck him in." His words were clear and stood
in the air for minutes.
They are in the air still.

When that moment of blinding violence comes,
in the bright color of crisp morning, your placid mind
serene before the ghastly display of scream and steel,
power and death, his sword will fall into the Void. - In
the pommel of your sword.

There is no doubt.

There on the pommel, or on the handle between the pommel and your fingers - he will be swallowed up.

There is no doubt.

But this is not the point of this form. The point of this form happens elsewhere, and without it, there is no point. - And without it, there is failure.

There are the secret words. The secret words that evoke the mind. That bring the secret power.

What were the secret words? The cadence put, the inference plied in those few mumbled syllables. Mumbled in the moment...

Pulled from the Earth, a universe explodes in a surge before one's eyes.

The bluest sky.

Stretching from the horizon, the whitest little clouds like snow flakes, catch the light.

Numbing color cascades. The mind is enraptured. Lives and earth gently caress as time is undone. The vision overtakes all worlds, its simplicity without bonds.

The rich brilliance of color bears down.

This is the moment. Only through this "Way," from these words, in this most delicately graceful, and long awaited now.

Only here can life be this way.

A coveted beauty. A treasured beauty.

A secret beauty.

An evocation of greatest human power, lucidity and art; hiding in the words. Awaiting this time. Waiting in secret.

- These are the words of Sensei.

Spring

I have just tired of many complex issues. - And relinquish the moment, and my word-processor, to the freedom of this spring afternoon,

- or maybe just a little R & R.

Sitting back, I tap out a quiet rhythm on my thighs. - Quickly a mating call from some anxious bug or bird returns an ardent message.

Two more calls and returns prove I'm the ~ Object of Romantic Desire ~

Well, of us two

...at least my friend is clearly focused!

Views

When was the first time? It was long before the three plump sparrows danced on the top of my shoes. Not the time under the sapling, either. With its delicate fronds and spring leaves filtering cool lemon sunshine on my little friends' curiosity, -as they danced on my shoulder. It wasn't then. I was accomplished, then.

It was when I was learning. When I figured out Sor. When I was sixteen.

I remember going to Joe Silva's (the one who started me playing guitar) who, by this time, was zealously guarding his hidden sources, the sheet music of the classics. In the middle of practice, he grabbed the paper up, ran and hid it under his bed. All things were hidden.

Perhaps, if it weren't for this tenaciously forced mystery, I may never have thought music such a big deal.

But I was driven. All of us were driven. It wasn't a question. The question couldn't occur to us. We were peers in this.

Correctness of music craft, sophistication of thought, phrasing and technique, all hidden. Guarded.

But design perfect position, I did. And design perfect attitude, I did.

And figure out Sor (the piece thrust under the box springs), I did. I did that this particular night.

When a sixteen year old is learning a classic guitar piece, the path is fraught with repetition. A process from which, sleep protected my parents.

The piece is a "Bachesque" thing in which low and high notes displace each other like the rearrangement of a child's building blocks.

Over and over, conquering mistake by mistake.

To play it once clear through, just once!

"Dah, dah, tah, -dah, tah, dah, -tah, dah, dah, -tah, tah, CLANK!"
Repeat: "Dah, dah, tah, -dah" Fun?

But I was driven.

11:30 became 1:30. Do I remember 3:30? It is without matter, I almost had it, several times. But always the "clank" of a mis-played note. Perfection only a flaw away.

Repeat. And repeat. And repeat. Until the notes and the flow separate in the meld. They are colored crimson in the air before me.

At last the Dominant comes flawlessly in resolve to the Fundamental, the conclusion of the long, long battle. Satisfaction overrides all discomfort at first attempts to push my back straight.

When I glance to the window, six feet to my left, the sky is emblazoned ice pink and thirteen large Ravens sit staring, inches from the glass.

I think that was the first time.

From My Kitchen Window

Bright stove light. Two excited eggs greet me from the
pan once again. A large woman and her daughter make
their way in the clear morning. The waves break silently
in the distance.

She is obese. Her daughter (a slip) is 11, wearing glasses,
bobbed hair, and plaid print.

She is at an age where her constant gooney expressions
are already a frustrating throw-a-way, ready to go.

Their exchanges are banter. Relevant to some common
aspect.

Going unseen and unheard, the banner of profoundest
austerity transcends their sweet musings.

Mother and daughter. This most ageless sovereignty;
here at play.

———————————————————

Flies
I was just watching a red-eyed fly that landed on my
lamp. You know, when you think about it, flies are always
cleaning themselves and preening - like cats. Cleaning
their wings and heads, with their little arms. -Flies are
clean!
                    (- who knew!)

Her Delicate Dream

Is her heritage Spanish or Native-American?

She pretends to have not been admiring the manne-
quined white satin wedding gown which dominates the
front display window.

She is clean and nicely dressed though obviously poor.
Her clear skin is marred with the discolor of a large
bruise under her right eye.

She is alone in the dark store alcove.

HUMBOLDT STATE UNIVERSITY

They told me about the printers in Gist. There are Laser Printers in Gist. Printer printers. REAL printers. - In Gist Hall.

They might card you in Gist.

"If they card you, you lie. Tell `em your Student Card is home, you'll bring it tomorrow. -Tomorrow never comes. Maybe change computer labs or lay low for a day. They won't card you. They never card, don't worry. Just watch out for Kate."

-words of Sabrina.

Still Gist is somewhere else and who needs it? Who wants CHANGE anyway. Not when there's comfortable status quo.

Well, there came a time for a printer-printer. A REAL PRINTER.

Once in Gist, though, my program couldn't speak printer-printer. For all the neat lettering, the spaces between words and between lines were mishap. But Gist has the regular printers plus a great variety of new comput-ers and different brands. Newer and nicer (and you can switch between printers).

So I switched labs - and frequented Gist.

As warned, there is a large woman in Gist. She runs Gist. She does not look friendly. Something in her gaze tells you it might be well to look in some other direction. Any other direction.

Kate has reddish-blonde, coarse hair and somehow Kate is Viking. Viking blood. Viking braids in Viking hair. A horned Viking hat adorns the preconstructed character-ization plainted by those disgruntled few forewarning me of Gist, and of Gist's Kate.

In Gist, I computed and I printed. I was productive and it was happy productivity. The sun streamed; common joy at flower.

Then it came.

Suddenly, Kate was at the head of the room. Everyone would be carded and anyone found card-lacking would be, "ASKED TO LEAVE."

A theatrically blank expression hid my frenzied despair. She had the door covered. No escape.

What about my stories? My papers? MY BOOK! ...MY ...MY?

One moment, warm sun, new equipment, engrossing creation; the next:

WHIRLPOOL OF AGONIES

Whirlpool of desks, flooring, printers, tumbling consoles, Kate; Kate's coarse blonde braids, Kate's eyes. Kate's eyes as on a turntable, one eye close in swinging `round and `round - the other in a wide orbit outside (the braids competing lazily).

I had been warned - Sabrina'd hissed her prophetic
truth. Dire dread fulfilled.

   Friday boldface:

GIST SHOOT-OUT! COMPUTER WARS AT HUMBOLDT
        Berserk teacher wields limitless power in
     crack-down rampage! Thwarted scum ejected!

- Kate cards EVERYBODY in a week.

I, the thwarted eject. Careerless. Humiliated. What for
the nectar of faceless anonymity, I must pace the dirge
of public derision.

Then: the unexpected. When it came time to present
myself, she met my free admission with the sweetest
warmth. Her cloudless spirit dispelled all apprehension.

A fine, if sad, parting.

Still lingering aftermath:
      And so I sit - clasping
      my branch, beady eyes affixed

                 ...on Gist Hall.

Dating Link

NOTE: A friend and her daughter excitedly read "The Dating-link" personals in the Times. She confessed having pursued dates therein the prior year.
When passing the Times the following day I thought to spice their reading a little. They ran weekly.
These quickly became hot discussions on local talk radio.

SUAVE, HANDSOME MALE SEEKS OUTGOING WOMAN
Ski, mountain-climb, scuba, bicycle-ride, romantic candlelit evenings. Athletic. Charismatic. Your perfect mate!
GREAT LOVER! (I know you) Sexual poetry. Surreal passion. - Millionaire!
ALL AROUND WONDERFUL PERSON - actually toad.
...wonderful toad. Received "Wonderful Toad Award!"
Everything your other dates WISH THEY WERE. Treat yourself.
                              WONDER TOAD

FAREWELL WONDERTOAD
Humboldt was saddened with news of the passing
of Wondertoad reported lost over the Andes.
Northcoast women offered condolences to family
and friends at Pierce Chapel. Rosary 8PM.

WONDERTOAD TRAGEDY
County reeling at sad passing of Wondertoad,
N. Calif's bright star, victim of Andes storm.
County-counsel acquiesces on memorial plaque.
Confused librarian, "This is worse than the earthquake."

WONDERTOAD DISCOVERED IN REMOTE VILLAGE!
Group of Eureka ladies sail this afternoon for Peru on
fact-finding mission. American Consul (Lima) advances
theory of mystery surrounding reluctance of locals in
releasing Humboldt native.

WOMEN MISSING IN WONDERTOAD SEARCH
Eureka Mayor and Dist. Attorney monitor events by phone.
Relatives spend rending all-nighter after jungle porters
return empty-handed. American Embassy demands poly-
graphs in diplomatic flap.

HUMBOLDT TOAD HELD AS TRIBAL-DEITY!
Peruvian military returns with bizarre claim - indigenous
traditions in turmoil. Second Indian group sets ransom on
Eureka women. American Ambassador angered when told,
"Go easy."

PARLAMENTARIO FOOT-DRAGGING DODGED
IN WONDERTOAD CASE
Ex-Junta boss accedes to U.S. pressure. Negotiations begin
this week on behalf of six missing Humboldt women. Ransom
reportedly $6MILLION! plus 2 dollars - "for frog."

F.L.N. SANDBAGS NEGOTIATION FOR WONDERTOAD!
Guerrilla group intercedes. Communique: "Government
inept." County church-raffles coordinated as Board of Sup's
draft rescue request. Bush Administration waffles on tariff
threat.

FATE OF EUREKA WOMEN - CENTER OF LATIN CRISIS
Mountain warlords' squeeze-play raises stakes in Wondertoad debacle. State Dept. emphasizes "TROUBLE IN CAPITAL-LETTERS." International tensions rise as Marines 2nd Div. positions off Peru coast.

FROG "HERO" IN SOUTH AMERICA!
Wondertoad plays risky trump-card in vortex of head-to-head multi-government power crush. Tribes drop differences and rally with vying guerrilla factions as old enemies unite to end Amazon de-forestation!

ORDEAL ENDS! "EUREKA SIX" RETURN TODAY
Women arrive at McKinleyville Airport tired but safe. Nobel Committee examines heroic role of Wondertoad in OZONE repair. Humboldt son to be honored at nostalgic mid-jungle bash tonight.

AIRFORCE 2 CARRIES HUMBOLDT HONOREE HOME
Wondertoad arrives on Presidential plane this afternoon. Delighted Times staff sees Nobel Laureate as "Dating Link" coup. Humboldt Sheriff, fearing traffic glut, asks that well-wishers use public transportation.

SUAVE, HANDSOME MALE SEEKS OUTGOING WOMAN
Ski, mountain-climb, scuba, bicycle-ride, romantic candlelit evenings. Athletic. Charismatic. GREAT LOVER! Millionaire! WONDERFUL PERSON - actually toad.
Received "Wonderful Toad Award" and Nobel Prize. Need date bad.

WONDERTOAD

(Our friend still can't get a date)

Tortoise

I had been afraid to fly, so we found a bus called "The Green Tortoise."

The captain of the Green Tortoise had long, graying braids falling to his belt. His passengers were long-haired youth - mostly. Fair = $80 to New York. New York via Arizona, Juarez and a Tennessee farm.

Four days east for a two week family Christmas. Then back.

A high platform made the seatless bus one long foam bed.

I immediately sought needed discomforts to support my intolerant mood, - griping all the way to Geronimo's hot-springs.

But there's something about hot-springs.

Arizona is dry. The still black night with its yellowed half-moon landing on the low hills. The air somehow swollen.

Story has a wounded Geronimo healing in secret.

The springs certainly healed me. The way to the Juarez Mercado, with its brilliant blankets and colorful embroidery was ease.

We showered in Tennessee.

After Christmas, the same crew met for the return. Down to Tennessee and over to Juarez.

The rendezvous in El Paso after another long day at the Mercado was slow. People waiting in the winter sun for stragglers.

Pulling their coats off for a stretch in the afternoon warmth were two gals from the trip out. They were probably college and had kept well-bundled and unnoticed, until now - at least by me.

I had to turn from her long stretch lest she see my struck gaze. She had learned a timid modesty to hide her almost perfect beauty.

I did my best to forget it.

When we came to the hot-springs, it was 11:30. Full-moon.

While others ate, I found my way to the springs.

These are several pools separated by brook. The hot one is 119 degrees. They fall around on the flat desert in a semi-circle. The final one has a run-off that drifts to a waterfall in a narrow six foot gorge. Its stream falls in a niche with a stone seat, really only big enough for one.

I don't know where my clothes were, but I found my-self gliding through the steaming gorge, the air a glisten-ing moon-lit gauze. Light clothed its walls in white. White rainbows from every point.

When I sat in the niche, she sat at the same time. I hadn't seen her until our skin touched. She said we'd share, with a laugh. Her friend stood disappearing in the steam two feet away. We may have said some friendly word or two. Our bodies pressed together under the heat of the foot-wide pour. Only the white steam and the liquid moon shimmering and pressing, like the thun-dering heat.

The dance of moments backed away, and the clear now enveloped us.

She was without pretense, "I feel drunk." I didn't need such an excuse, but we didn't know each other ...and I knew she would have to return to her life. - And I to mine.

So we waited, figures in alabaster - in the moon-silver, swollen air.

RICK and KAY

I didn't drink, so my date and I were in the front. I was driving. Rick and Kay, and Rick's best friend and his date were in the back. We were all dressed nicely. - All dressed up.

We parked on a dark, empty road and they all got soused.

It was fun til Rick poked me in the eye. I had made some joke about telling Kay some secret. I remember his head behind his rapidly growing finger, "If you do!" - He didn't mean to poke my eye. It was closer than he thought.

To everyone's dismay, his friend swung the rear door next to him and proceeded to get sick. I guess the idea appealed to Rick.

Not occurring to him that he sat by the left window, he lurched across both dates to join his friend at the far door. General panic exploded from the backseat. Calls and screams echoed from our rocking auto before the inevitable sound of his enjoined chorus confirmed completion of the threat, and alerted me not to breath through my nose.

Unfortunately, in their tangled struggle, Kay's hand had become trapped directly under Rick's mouth.

Ahh, the teenage years.

MONEY

I was thirteen and had been coerced into my first job, working as a delivery boy at my dad's shop. COPY CATS was a blueprint, photostat, off-set print house in San Francisco.

Blueprint shops have a pervasive ammonia odor, one never forgets. I was on the delivery bench with older city kids, and adults. You went by bike or foot. Swinging doors allowed us past the order-desk and long entrance way.

The wide, flat sidewalks were alive with the same energetic bustle as the shop. The smell of cigars and cigar stores competed in the rustle of people, traffic and the constant gurgle of cable-car cables running through rail-slats in the street.

An invisible overhead lantern held the promise of sunshine, but never quite got all the way down. And a stench of hot metal from some hidden somewhere clashed with the echoes of car horns and trolleys.

I spent an afternoon loading technical drawings into the gasping port of a gigantic blueprint machine with a friendly Filipino print trimmer named Gus, who sported a huge pompadour. He confided he used to make delicate little spit bubbles in class and gently blow them off his tongue to drift in the air and eventually soak the pretty blonde ponytail in the seat just ahead. He had become quite an artist at it.

At the end of the first pay period I had earned a check for $29.00 - which I cashed into $1.00 bills.

This was my first money. I counted it on the rug, over and over.

What do we do with our first money?

I took my friends to Spreckles Ice Cream and treated all.

THE BREAD MESS ON THE FRONT PORCH
IS NOT MY FAULT

I took the old sour-dough from the refrigerator and placed it out for the birds. After a short period I heard a loud commotion. Looking out, I saw a mass of little birds in a huge punch-out. Bread crumbs flying.

I went out and, except for two combatants wrestling in the now disintegrating loaf, all heads turned my way. To the dismay of their embarrassed peers, the grimacing pair made odd grunting sounds. A bird foot on one's face, the latter grasping his foe about the neck with an outstretched wing.

Presently, (the sudden silence, a message of unerring import) they realized I was watching, shook off and got up. These two avoided my gaze and couldn't look me in the eye.

They all knew they were caught, but nobody knew what to say. Their nervous glances seemed to offer, "Well, what do ya expect, WE'RE BIRDS!"

All at once, they began looking about in different directions, as if on a train platform, awaiting a car. - Obvious pretense.

I didn't want to appear stupid, so, to their relief, I ended my monotonous censure and stepped in. We all looked at each other briefly; and with nothing further forthcoming, I closed the door with a soft click.

Immediately a thrashing ensued, but now somewhat muted.   -Bob

Let me tell you a little story...

We wish to travel to our children on Mars.
We pack a few things, excitedly, and tell the NET our
plan. The elevator takes us to a shuttle.

Inter-city or inter-planetary travel is very fast - vehicles
and occupants are an integrated charge-field. You feel no
acceleration. Its just like being in your kitchen.

In this world, you can do anything you want. You can
pursue any art. Any science.

You can do nothing.

Since you don't need to die, you can stop. You can enter
a dream and no dream state and let the present pass on
by. You can come back when everything is new. You can
have a new adventure.

You can decipher unknown segments of unknown ge-
nome. You can pursue skiing.

Your body looks like a 32 year old. It runs like a 27 year
old. Your mind is limitless. Your abilities are limitless.

Men do not fear women. Women do not fear men.

Women play no games, there's no need. She has no lim-
its. All men are perfect beings. - All wonderful people.
All women are perfect beings.

Every relationship is easy. Women are what ever they
wish. Men are finally every thing that the masculine gift
can give. All talent and ability. And all wonderful people.

Women are whatever they wish.

You can be sexual. Or not. It's OK. Anything is OK because everything is possible. And everyone is fine. All
fine beings.

No one wastes their time, now that it is limitless. How
strange to think that when it is proscribed, people do
nothing but waste it.

I am glad our parents took the resolve to grow from the
squalor of the dark ages.

WAITING ON THE BUS-STOP BENCH

He has a knotted fleece beard and hair to match,
poking from under his multi-speckled knit beret.

He is sewing some tattered rag, cigarette hanging
from his lip.

His second-hand smoke has just jarred my attention
from reading.

At first, an intrusion, but now something else.

Suddenly it's Seals Stadium, San Francisco. 1952.

The odors mellow and coalesce
                    ...from another world

TEA

The tea master and her guest sit quietly before the lake.

Tailored blossoms cling to a vased sprig, - and young saplings jut from the green slope.

On the left bank, a clutch of pine stretch over the water. Glistening gold catches each little ripple, and each blade of grass.

...And long strands of silk wave silently from the pines - far, far above.

A little-one has crawled with her brothers and sisters to the top of the pine, a pilgrimage...
- planned before time.

There, she lets out her silk... In an ageless dance - with old Father Wind

For the tree and the wind...

live together

Her silk and the sweet air know each other. Demanding Father Wind wants enough, and she holds on

Life depends on her strength, on her silk
...and on the Wind

The silk and Father Wind are one, - and always have been
...And they want her

It is her moment

An ancient and renewed moment... for her, and all her
kind
            ...all that were, and all that will be...
      She is overcome ...and finally tugged from the
tree.

She will leave our tea master, and her guest
                              to their delicate afternoon

She will leave this country

She will ride the jet stream   ...to other worlds

She will meet her lover 10,000 feet above the ground

She will meet animals that have never lived on the earth

She will ride with the lucky...
                  And lonely travelers,

In a sea of pollen and debris   ...and lost ships

High on the misty edge   ...of the Universe

THIGER

Jeff Thigpen was the star.
He was the star in Kindergarten

He was the star in third grade
He was the star in 6th

He was best ...at baseball
                 ...at basketball
                 ...at kickball

After grade school, he was best at football
                    (Park Elementary had had asphalt)

He was the best at studies ...best at math
He had the best grades. Park: 24 Xs, High School -
straight As.
                 This was different from Sheldon, the worst
student, with 24 Us.

Jeff was the head of the head clique. The rarefied air.

He taught me three things:

   One - Take up the Nabisco bag in both hands, and
crush the Shredded Wheat biscuits within - before pour-
ing into the bowl.

   Two - Put the entire lb. of bacon in the skillet and allow to separate of its own.

   Three - Roast marshmallows artistically by teasing the
flame until the candy swells to a softball-size chiffon puff
with a delicate brickle crust.

HAKATA Bay in CHIKUZEN
　　　MOKU-SHURAI The Invasion of the Mongols

KAMIKAZE "The Divine Wind"

On August 15, 1281, KAMEYAMA-JOKO, the retired father
of Emperor GO-UDA, appeared before AMATERASU "The
Divine Goddess of the Sun" in ISE asking her intervention
on behalf of Japan.

900 Korean ships with 10,000 infantry and 17,000 sailors
had ferried 15,000 Chinese and Mongol troops to rendezvous at IKI Island with the 3,500 ship Chinese "Yang-tze"
task-force of 60,000 navy carrying 100,000 soldiers to
conquer the Land of the Gods.

Six and half years before, the 150 ship first invasion had
thrashed against the coast in a storming November night
to the loss of 13,000 lives.

This was summer - the well-planned, long awaited summer.

A sea of angry boats and garish streamers imposed hid-
eous clarity to the excited echoes of drums and horn, -
filtering over the flat, naked water.

The Japanese had prepared six and half years.
HOJO TOKIMUNE's coordinated national muster stood
ready but outnumbered on its fifteen foot, 25 mile wall
protecting HAKATA from the waves and this vast spectacle
painted across everyone's eyes.

Moving effortlessly from the horizon, a small black dot
appeared in the cloudless sky.

- Searching a station just above the throng, it stretched dark fingers without wait.

A huge and deafening still swallowed their noisy clamor as the ocean and its ships began to leap in eerie silence.

Then the leaves started rattling...

Foretelling the deep growl that shook trees before its violent thunder hit with howling rage. Flags were pulled from standards. And warriors clung for the moaning earth - just to watch.

Careening ships were pitched on crags or dragged away. Swamped wrecks rolled over, and over each other in the boiling sea; - grinding the vessels to splinter wood.

The sight made men drunk, some sat numb.

AMATERASU allowed three lives to return the news to Kublai-Khan.

All travelers know...

Perhaps they haven't looked ...but travelers know.

The day of departure ...or the twilight before,
                                    it hits them.

They are gone from this place... Gone from their
loves, gone from their life.

They are gone from this place, and all those they
know - or wish to know

They all
        are in comfort,
                    busying after themselves - pursuing them-
selves,

    ...while the traveler prepares

The traveler will be forgotten
So the day for departure is hollow.
Our traveler is hollow. The air is hollow.

How is it then for the soldier?

Is he forever disconnected?

SEIROGAN

We have a mild flu. My friend, Yoshi, is attempting his cure with SEIROGAN. SEIROGAN means "Conquer Russia" Drops (or Grains). -Looks like bat-guano. Smells like kerosine-smoked jerky. Every Japanese kid knows this stuff.

I've tried to compete with Chicken Noodle Soup. Yoshi is un-moved. It cured the 1905 Imperial Army, it cured the boys in WWII, it cured his parents and it will cure him.

SEIROGAN has several ingredients, faithfully adhered to since Port Arthur. Among them, the label divulges plant extracts, common "Naturiums" such as sodium carbonate and main cure-all: Creosote and Root-X!

Yes... the wonders of modern medicine.

THE DANCE

Once I hiked up the mountain we lived on, way out
in the country. Far up beyond where I had ever been.
I found myself alone on the rolling mountain top in
golden, end-of-the-year grass.

Just a couple of bush-sized evergreens and the empty
still of the afternoon.

Suddenly a beautiful whistling drifted in. A dance of
many voices piping rich and husky tones filled the air.
Large ravens were running and circling in a moving, energetic pack that twisted along the ridge.

I knew instantly this was secret ritual and that I might
eavesdrop on something not allowed human ears. I hid
under the branches as they came directly over.

A whirling symphony of lyrical fluting and joyous excitement sent long, brilliant ribbons of smooth color curling
from their wing-tips and a woody, percussive staccato
echoed like coconut drums.

Bright yellow, green and red streamers strung through
the sky...

In the peace of cool morning

A blackbird flits through the trees, 80 yards off.

Did he know I was taken by him - that this moment was of him?

He came to me. - He is missing a foot.

He raised his good foot & stood on the stump. - A learned declaration?

He has jumped to the bench, inches from my shoulder - we, eye to eye

Being ready...

Yesterday, I was visiting a gal-friend (if I can call her that) who owns a small espresso spot under an awning-covered stand on the outer main drag of the downtown area.

The downtown, at this time, has its unsavory elements. The unsavory side can weigh upon the landscape.

But this is a great gal, with a nice place - which draws the brighter, more industrious crowd of people.

We were attempting conversation between the regular flow of nab-and-run coffee enthusiasts when a newer blue truck stops in about a hundred feet away. A guy jumps out and runs up. The car pulls around to the stand exit. Its driver has nervous, darting expressions but stays in the car.

The guy before us is lean, - dressed in unwashed clothes. His skin seems taut and dark, yet his conversation has an odd, misfitting friendliness. He is "talky". He says he has to watch her, - he must see if she makes cappuccino good enough, as his has to be "just so." He wants to know how her coffee machine is holding up. He asks about business. He thinks she will do good at this location. He is looking around to the right, and to the left.

I step around and check the license. It's out of state and a steaming cup of coffee sits in the open truck-bed.

He leans over to look behind the counter, to the left and to the right, talking all the while. Something is in his pocket. He puts his hand in and out of his pocket, raising and lowering a small squarish shape that is within. His talk is designed to keep us following some conversational line.

I position myself so that I can try whatever I might have to if he pulls a gun out of that pocket. I will try to crush his windpipe with a quick blow, if allowed the time. Otherwise, it will be wrestling with a gun.

I look him up and down and think to myself, "this guy will probably kill me."

He is standing by the door and asks if I'm the guard. I say "no, just a friend..."

SPEED

Makoto phones. He tells me he's going to have sword exhibition at the Cherry Blossom Festival in Japan Town that next week. He needs an associate for proper explanation to the people.

I, of course, haven't done sword drawing for about two years and explain I'm completely out of shape, etc. This doesn't matter because he is completely out of shape too. That's why I must help. It's OK because nobody'll be there anyway. Just two rusty sword guys.

"Just do some SHOMANs" is how I remember his good-by.

SHOMAN is an IAI sword draw where the blade is brought in a full swing directly over the head. It is the most powerful cut and practicing it makes the most powerful swordsmen.

"1000 SHOMAN a day"

"If you do 1000 SHOMAN a day, you are strongest swordsman. This is oldest rule."

The sword starts from an extension all the way down the back, parallel with the backbone. The shoulder blades splay, your elbows arc toward the sky. Your stomach muscles grab your chest. From the side, the veneer of sword steel swinging a broad swath through the air appears like the shell of a snail. Wider in back and pulling tightly to the front.

The arms twist the handle as if ringing a towel. You exert

full pressure, with the spirit of lifting a Sherman Tank to save your child. - After all, your life's supposed to be on the line.

Five of these and you're wondering when the purple dots 'll stop whirling.

I remember doing many when I did sword, but now I'm out of shape.

(Still, you're going to be on stage, pal. - Time to start hump'in!)

So I practice. I practice all day. I practice all week. I practice so much a certain part of my forearm distends abnormally. - And hurts abnormally!

By show day, my arm is weak. My arm is painful. My form is shaky - literally.

I have driven into the city. I am in my HAKAMA and GI, sitting dutifully in the mad crush of a vibrant and frenzied San Francisco Cherry-Blossom Festival. Bright color and excited children swirl across the eyes. There is no let up.

Finally Makoto arrives. His martial arts gear is different. His friends with the Japanese theater group have supplied him the full bearance of a seventeenth century RONIN. The print of his tattered garment is brighter than these kids'. - Headband. Hair. - This guy LOOKS REAL!

We set up and a crowd gathers. - A large crowd gathers. The old, the young, women with babies; other martial artists. Shop keepers.

I whisper, "I'm out of shape." Makoto whispers back, "it's OK, me too." - I kind of give him a nod, a kind of questioning nod. (I'm kind of questioning all right, - what am I doing here?)

But Makoto needed my help. He'd have to have gotten up here without any help. Without any support. He started me on sword. - Esprit de corps! We'll make it through this.

Makoto does a long bit to the swelling audience about the Samurai, the martial arts, the martial tradition, modern keepers of the flame, etc. And then turns it over to me for the first routine.

I fumbled my draw and felt my face redden at the close of my first shaky cut. I remember the snicker that crept to an old man's face enjoying the spectacle.

Lots of fun! - And I only had three more to go.

One was so-so, the rest...
                Lots a fun.

Finally it was poor Makoto's turn. I tried to tell myself the pressure was off a little, maybe we weren't actually there. Maybe there wasn't this sea of faces. Maybe they would all watch him now.

Makoto may have said something. His body disappeared into a small metallic ball. He did three or four, maybe four or five cuts - and a clean return within one second.

The old man's face lit with pride.

I was stunned.

(- I was pissed!)

POOR MAKOTO!?!!

- I didn't want to be here anyway!

We were to trade places. And as we passed, our eyes glanced right to each other and I heard the whisper, "Three hundred a day."

—————————————————————

SPEED2: REVENGE
[Continued from previous story]

One of the fun things you can do at sword demonstration is offer to cut an apple off the head of a three year
old. To prove the mother's fears unfounded, I'm supposed to stop Makoto, suggesting we first use a Styrofoam head as a test. Of course, the styrofoam head eats
it.

We didn't have styrofoam at this Cherry Blossom demonstration but a total stranger took the toddler's place in
stiff seizan and full confidence. Makoto'd been great but
this was mind boggling. Makoto and I just looked each
other but kept straight faces. This demonstration was
proving full of surprise. Makoto declined the man's kind
offer, but what with enough bananas and apples, and
Makoto's - HEIGHTENED SKILLS - we trudged through.

(Three hundred SHOMANs...)

Makoto had told me we were to appear twice. The second was to be in two weeks at the Festival finale.

(Two weeks... in two weeks, there, buddy)

We bid smiling farewells. In two weeks. We'd see each
other in two weeks.

Two weeks...

Did I practice?

Luckily I had the perfect place, a pre-Victorian church
with twenty foot ceilings. Built in 1868 by the Druids,

it had two floors, each a large room with a large empty floor.

- Two DOJOs!

I only needed one.

Two weeks. Night and day, flashing steel and KIAI. A slapping of the floors. A great slapping of the floors. The air pulsated, the windows shuttered.

Spouse gained resolve but the cats left.

...And spouse started shopping alot.

But I got good. I got REAL good.

I could smear the horizon with both hands. Clean returns with both hands, - smooth as glass.

I cut a candle so both sides were left burning.

...And I got fast. I got REAL fast.

I worked up three KATA. Two were carefully tame. But the third...

In the third KATA, I am attacked by eight opponents. This of course requires two swords.

  (- Eight opponents require two swords)

Let's see, how did that go... I'm attacked from the front but a second attacks from the right. This doesn't require two swords, but a third comes from behind. His sword gets clasped by the guard of my short-sword and he is led through with his own momentum, pulling him further than he allowed. While pushing him, sword guard to sword guard on a line at the left, I step around to the right and cut his back. Then the rest of them attack and of course that's when the action really begins. The audience will be impressed. The audience will be REAL impressed.

Makoto WILL BE impressed. That old man will be impressed.

I'm impressed. Spouse is impressed ...but the cats - are gone.

Nothing matters, for the day of SWEET REVENGE has arrived.

My mind is calm. My spirit is boundless. My energy - contained. Smooooth. Ready.

We drive to the city.

I wait again in the still festive but now noticeably exhausted wane of the yearly party. Paper and liter stroll on marble walkways while people chase after voices and echoes. Through the clutter and clatter I see Makoto running up.

N-O-W. Now, IT'S MY TURN.

He's dressed in a suit and bounds the stairs.

"Ah, so sorry, called off." And runs away.

Paradise

It was a time of robust productivity

and care-free happiness...

Driving through the city, on our way home, we found a
new and special delight insisting, for us, a regular stop
to the stand of "Gelato's San Francisco Italian Ice Cream"
on Parnassus.

~ Coffee Mocha ~

A deeply rich, espresso ice cream - with chunks of semi-
sweet, cracked chocolate.

Gelato's teases you with samples proffered in one-inch
cups and miniature spoons.

Their full array of flavors and colors included the multi-
hued, Italian Spumone, which was of course, marvelous...

but the *~ Coffee Mocha ~*

...this was heaven. Truly heaven.

Slowly, in the midst of our euphoria, a disagreement
emerged which revolved around this singular, and most
highly crucial, question: Was the coffee ice cream, - as
presented in the beloved, Coffee Mocha, a better coffee
ice cream than that of store bought
                    Haagen Dazs Ice Cream - ???

This battle raged with continuing frequency at each of

our many Gelatos' stops. Accompanying friends were
drawn in and occasional strangers would find delight in
voicing their often absurd opinions.

The gauntlet thrown, a bet was staked and a date set.
We picked up a Haagen Dazs on the way in.

Fully fifteen people grouped in the twilight before the
famous sidewalk ice cream bar.

I can tell you, in all of my life, I was never so fully confident of such an obvious outcome as on the corner of
Parnassus and Stanyan, San Francisco, that evening.

Everyone was dished their appropriate ration and all
eyes fell together

   as we tasted, first the one
       ...and then the other

maymoon

OK, The Great Western is held at the LA fairgrounds, -
weather was fantastic.

The sun had baked a hot pillow for one of those full
moons where everything just floats.

At the height of spring, it's the fulcrum of the whole year
- and the evening is made of syrup.

Everything moves slow... no reason to think, it's useless.

Dreamy old moon's happiest smile, swells across the sky

_____

That day you walked through gun-show madness,
    building after building.
Each as big as any in the country.
    It's just like Disney Land, only it's Gun Show - times 6.

Six exposition buildings plus the Great Hall,
    people and stall-packed broad-walks and boulevards.

Different music and sounds blend
        as bands play and food vendors try to keep pace.
    Melting ice cream, soda pop, beer, hot dogs,
        sandwiches - Mezco food,
                German food, Indian food, hamburgers.

You couldn't walk three steps in one direction.
    Packed. Lines for food, lines for the john, lines for the
phones,
            while fanning spouses on recess, and smokers
                            compete for the shade.

Gunslingers and cowboys, Rebs and Yanks with stars
and bars and union jack. Doughboys and GI foot-soldiers
walk between tanks and stagecoach, cannons and anti-
aircraft.

Endless displays in towering racks and glass cases,
stacked and spread, piled and hanging. Every possible
collectable: stamps, coins, ivory, American Indian, cow-
boy, Old West, militaria of any era from every country,
Civil War; tables of dueling pistols and six-shooters.
Pocket knives and Bowie knives. Secret Agent weapons
from past or present, swords from any era - any place;
pirate stuff, ship and marine. Brass; ancient clocks and
watches. African spears and shield, European armor,
Japanese armor, Persian daggers. Roman swords, swords
from Polynesia; Chinese weapons, halberds, spears,
axes, bows and cross-bows; glassware, Korean ceram-
ics, ancient Egypt. Samurai swords and religious relics,
a mummified hand, a sultan's armor; the dagger of a
Caliph and his turban, too. A jeweled sword stolen from
the tomb of an Asian king.

Loads of stuff. Loads of stuff.

Mid-morning

It's her girl friend. She's rushed and excited, and blended perfectly, her surprise at this unexpected find. Instantly, they poured uncontained delight and whispers into the bedroom. Besides the BIG question, and where did she meet me, they took a moment exchanging their other news and their day's planned adventures.

Her charged excitement unwaned, we were introduced and the three of us finished our toast and strawberry breakfast.

A letter

I'll tell you one. I was in this college sports bar. I was still
39 and went there to play pool (I was good at that - it
was another of those "Natural" deals). Anyway - there
was this guy in there. He had long hair drooping forward from each side of a blue knit cap and a long, full,
soft brown/blonde mustache. He quickly showed a
smooth, easy humor that you just have to take right to.
He seemed to be two or three years older than I and
had some great jokes in between the little observations
that come into your head just as he is pointing them out.
This guy, you like. Immediately. We played pool back
and forth for about an hour, all the while having an all
around great time.

Suddenly a smiling gal is there, very friendly and talking
at a rather high rate, but pleasant. She seems to know
him. They very quickly acknowledge having seen each
other at the bank where she works. He would see her
when she helped him at the "Commerce" line. He's a
professional fisherman.

We three were talking and friendly - she flirting, not too
much, and generally giving us both an obvious approval.
It began to appear conspicuously that more was con-
densing from the earlier informalities.

Amidst the bar clamor and chaos, in a closer and closer
triangulation, I saw her, close on my left, ask over to him,
close on my right, "How old are you?" He replied, "27" -
to which she said, "Oh great! I'm 26!" And then both, in
perfect concert, swung their smiling faces around in to
me, saying in unison, "And how are old are you?"

Something about this vision made me know, to decide carefully, as my mouth began to open, "thir-rty... - two."

To which her whole countenance darkened and a win-tery cold fell across her words, "Oh-h-h... I-I- did-n't kno-o-w - that... " He looked surprised but was following her - their figures seemed to break up like ships leaving a tie-up in high seas.

So you know I was LOOKIN' good, anyway!

_____

The Perfect Crime

We had play-money - and matches. The long deserted
vacant lot was over-grown with large eucalyptus leaning lazily. Its surrounding fence had an old decorative
railing clinging along the top, and the ruddy ground had
scruffy straw with the same lazy sway as the trees. The
lifeless stalks hugged each other in the cool afternoon.
They were the trunks of a jungle forest hiding the secret
cave of dinosaurs; - which we decided to smoke out. And
we had the perfect tools. We stuffed the gopher hole
with paper money and lit it up. Of course, the dry grass
caught fire and quickly got away from us.

Panicked, we ran for it, but taking circuitous paths to
our respective homes to change clothes and pretend
we were somewhere else. I put on my white bucks with
it's thin black belt as the fire engines rang through the
neighborhood. When I crossed back over to my friend's,
his whole family was out back standing on the fence
looking at the fire department raking the smoking and
blackened rear property.

No one knew and we never talked about it.

Smoking

I was smoking cigarettes when I was at camp with the other boys. We would go out into the forest.

Once, they called an unprecedented: "Count! In three minutes!". This was a 'never before' and we knew we were busted. We ran as fast as boys can run. Through the trails and behind the tents. We charged into our respective domiciles and grabbed for the nearest tooth-paste. Pulling the tube from the shelf, I squirted it into my mouth just as the counselor came into the dorm.

It had no taste.

I looked at the print:
   Brylcreme - *"A little dab will do ya"*

The Spider

I was sick. My home, at the time, was a converted step-van with a blown engine and a skylight above the bed.

This was many years ago and not unusual for the time, as anyone who could live in our artist's community, lived there anyway they could - but that's another story.

I had been sick for weeks. In a crevice between the insulation and the sky-light glass, a jumping spider retained its abode. One could argue just who is the master in such quarters.

He was black with slight red spots across his back. He hunted flies like a cat hunts mice. Jumping spiders do not make webs. They use silk to anchor themselves when they jump.

The flies would land up around the window and he would head out.

Just like a cat - he'd cautiously dart from one frozen position to another. Wh-whack! The ensuing 'last-struggle' was a buzzing-ball, swinging from his single line about two or three inches from the roof.

He'd drag them up into his crevice.

These were great entertainments from my vantage point directly beneath. He didn't get them all, so these were tense contests. And, having become my friend, I was his admirer and greatest rooter. (How is it, my number of friends remains steady so? - Nevermind)

I noticed his spots were slowly and steadily becoming

more. More red spots, and bigger. They grew until, slowly, the spots took over his entire back, becoming a full field of red velvet.

He was now a red-backed jumping spider.

One day he failed to come out. You can guess my concern, and worry, as my favorite friend did not come out to play. All day and into the late afternoon - which then became night.

He didn't come out the next day.

Nor the next.

- I had lost my friend.

On the forth day, in the midst of my morning meal, ten thousand babies swarmed from the opening. My euphoric cheer climaxed when, after some moments, SHE came out resting on the ledge - babies darting everywhere. She looked down, exhausted and happy, her eyes shining while I looked up, exhausted and happy, my eyes shining too.

Two cry-babies in the woods.

For Rent

I remember hearing about a place for rent - "Go out to Lagunitas, there's an empty place just up the back road"

We drive out to Lagunitas, drive into the small main road that follows around and up the hillside.

A house appears on the right. We get out and walk down to the empty porch. There's an odd smell, an old smell. The door is open.

She starts poking around in other parts of the house while I poke around in the kitchen.

There are few things left. We join up in the front room where a once nice dresser has intricate fret-work coming apart over its surface. It had been artfully made and seems completely unique.

We turn and walk together down the hall. A chair sits directly in the way. On the chair, a mirror is propped to face it's reflector to the back. A bullet sits upright in the center of the seat.

We walk around it and come to a small bedroom. There is a small spring mattress under a large, open window. The fall leaves have been blown in across a full set of women's under-clothes that are laid out as if having been worn. The garter clasps hold the stockings which stretch away from the limp panties. There are some kind of wadded and ritually burned material filling the bra cups.

The air was stale and dank.

We just walked out and drove off. I don't think we talked about it right away.

the naked eye

Yoshi said he made it through college by doing pencil sketches.

"Hey, that's great Yoshi."

Yoshi says he's gonna do something for me to see.

"Hey, great."

Yoshi gets a drawing pad, several pencils and hand-held pencil sharpeners.

A couple days later, I see the vague form of a woman. It might be a face and torso - and are those wings on her back? -(!)

I'm doing important computer-art for our up-and-coming Newsletter, so this stuff, whatever it is, doesn't matter.

I notice, in passing, the woman's face has a 40s look to it. Full lips, swept hair. But as I say, I'm doing important stuff and this is just something Yoshi is piddling with.

Later, Yoshi gets risque by adding rather voluptuous breasts - (but hey, - whatever!)

We all fly off to some city and return - time passes. I notice the drawing-pad on the kitchen counter. I open it.

She could be a dream.

It's not just the twist piping and machinery she has for internal organs, seen through her transparent ribs like some MC Escher drawing, it's the other-worldly textures and nuance of light from impossible dimension. Graphite lays like spackle.

Artist and window reflect at sweeping angle from each eyelash. Curved reflections create the pores of her skin and each delicate hair of her cheek.

Her mysterious eyes are jewels - of hidden worlds.

- Yoshi doesn't wear glasses.

_____

Life
Everyone sits around not taking life seriously.
It's amazing.

San Francisco

There was this dope dealer. A black dude, in the early seventies. Someone rolled up on him with a shotgun down on O'Farrell.

His lawyer, Tony S. from the radical days, got together with old friends, Jerry Garcia and another for a wake in a room at the Jack Tar. Commiserating on his not unexpected demise, they shook the lead pellets out of his ashes, mixed in his remaining pound and half of coke, - and snorted him up.

The Stand-off

It was the last day in December and there had been a fight in my apartment-complex. Police cars filled the parking lot like beached tuna.

The combatants were corralled separately. Different groups of officers arbitrating their guy for peace.

After endless negotiation, the antsy moment for the obligatory hand-shake finally arrived. The two were pushed into proximity.

Just as palms clasped, scores of individuals exploded from every neighbor door rapid-firing guns into the night. The cops hunkered to firing positions. Barrels leveling across every hood.

The whites of widening eyes noticeably studded all silhouettes as the neighborhood froze before this sea of law enforcement. They all scrabbled back inside.

One cop snickered, " -It's New Year's..."

India

Ran into the worst Monsoon on record. We walked out
looking for my friend's 6 1/2 year old son, stuck in the
missing school bus. It got chest-deep in 30 minutes.
Through the din, a few submerged headlights showed
the surface carpeted in a forest of five inch water-spouts.
We struggled up onto the porch of his good friends and
watched the water rise. -Didn't know if his son or wife
were ok until 3 in the morning.

1200 died; and as many cattle, which littered the streets
for a week.

Richard Sullivan

I remember him in second grade. He had straight, evenly
dark red hair which was easily slicked by the 50s hair
products. He was in his little chair behind the kid's-size
oak long table. I was across. We were purposely irritat-
ing the substitute teacher by making gyrations every
time she turned away. Richy would arch his back, sticking
his chest way out - and I'd do the same. She keep chasing after us - we'd keep the arching motion going and
she kept getting riled. He'd laugh with a huge grimacing smile, then snap back to placid - it was out and out
rebellion. We were in cahoots.
He lost his life to a sniper in Vietnam.
He was a wonderful person, smooth, easy personality.
Smart - he'd have had a wonderful, successful business
with wonderful successful kids.
He'd be a grandfather now -

Christy at Four
I had seen her before - but this was really the first meeting.

I think it was Barbie she had asked for - but it was an introductory present and could have been anything. I said it was in the box on the floor in the next room.

This was an empty box that would be my cleaver tease.

I peeked around the door to witness her confused frown.

Upon opening the top, she lithely bounded across the hardwood and up into my lap. Her big blue orbs became the whole world while I heard the calculated massage of her bright little babytalk: "How can a BIG person like you, do that to a little person like me!"

She tickled me with both hands, hard like an adult, and bounced away giggling.

Christy B Fore
She was just three, and sat in the sun against the open front-door. When her mother turned back - she was gone.

The while mom was flipping out, she had snuck away, up the block around back.

In fact, about three blocks up to the main drive liquor store - where all the candy was. The manager found her loading up.

She had the same allowance as her sisters and was purse

in-hand.

The manager became concerned and called police. Accosted by the cookies, she informed them that she would not be giving out her mommy's name nor phone number and she would not be getting into a stranger's car including the officer's.

Of course, the adults plied her with goodies - she, deftly steadfast.

Coincident with when she knew she could carry no more, it was time for them to think they had outsmarted and could then be allowed her mommy's number.

Besides, it was time to go home.

Christy, Busted

She's been gone long enough to go looking. We find her half way back from the river and brandishing a mask of flustered consternation. This expression tells of things hidden. Things to be found out; - to be inquired after.

She stares up, feet planted, her body and the world dangling from her eyes. Both fists and both pockets bulge. The pockets are moving. The skin between her fingers moves.

She stares up.

"What's in your hands, Christy?"

Christy: "Nothing... "

Roads

In the winter, the Bolinas Mesa looks like a WWI battle-
field. The Somme, with jagged trenches from the many
battles; - pitting truck against mud.

Racing for the sea, we take a hard left to stay in the run
and swing sideways at full throttle. Muddy spires arc
to the sky while burnt tires and steam hold the barrel-
ing head long course up the road-slick to a high ground
safety. The neighbors came out to cheer.

Other areas are relatively solid. Cars snake between
wide, one and two inch deep puddles in easy swings.

March came and I rounded Cedar St in a slow roll
through a glassy brown swath pooled on good, rocky
hard-tac.

The tire went down. Water bubbled in.

I pulled myself through the window and stepped off onto
the road-side, one foot away as the car disappeared
under the surface.

That's the last I saw of that car.

_____

Doors

I was twenty-something and had just broken up with my
live-in. Nose diving, it was get a job or become the stav-
ing artist.

As I had found previous refuge some three years prior as
a pot-washer in a nunnery, it was natural to find myself
applying at the exclusive Mountain Meadows Country
Club tucked on a private drive near the Marin Reservoir.

Accorded invader status by staff, I was waived toward
the rear door and told to "see the Head Chef."

Outside was the empty still of the employees parking
area. Small white garages sat parallel along the asphalt
which seemed to interrupt the soft chill of the morning.

Making sure I had not misunderstood, she redirected:
"last on the right"

Walking down, sure enough, there is an open door on
the last little building. Within, a large, actually rotund
but solid man in a rumpled undershirt and lax suspenders came into view. He sat, nearly filling the mattress
that nearly filled the windowless room. The only furnish-
ings were an integrated toilet and shower attached to
one wall.

With a vaguely foreign accent, he asked what experience I had - which I relayed with all the interview charm
I could muster.

He started shaving and talking little. I noticed pictures
adorning one side of the door. The nine foot ice sculp-

ture, in one, caught my eye. It rose from a rolling platform, in front of which stood the chef amidst an adoring
crowd which included the Queen of England. Another
picture had Elizabeth Taylor. Another was on the Riviera,
probably Monaco. I noticed Grace Kelly. There were
other pictures.

After a few moments, he asked if I was an artist. I began,
"I play music... " Immediately he seized forward, "I'll
make you the greatest Chef in the world." With a grand
sweep of his hand, "I'll start you on salads - "

I can't remember how I handled it from there. It isn't
every day the greatest Chef in the world offers to make
you the greatest Chef in the world. I had this idea about
being the greatest rock star in the world (not for a moment guessing life's strange turns).

But it was an honor to be seen as a probable protege. -
All in 25 minutes.

Back to the Land

It sits tucked into the hillside, evergreens hugging close
down. Long shelves carpeted in a sea of golden chaff.
The house had sat in the middle, under the standing oak,
between two long gardens. An out-building once stood
along the drive, where the cars and kids ran around.
They were in their twenties. He worked in the sun wearing a derby hat with miner's sweats and she had long
tumbling curls.

Easter cometh

Coordinating local markets, some 90 dozen eggs are rounded together for the Saturday boil up. Families gather and strategies engage.

Hissing and spitting caldrons watch stained kids dunk color. Gathered groups marshal the floor where donated baskets and green straw are put with stuffed animals and gummy bears.

Drawing lines and arguing routes, the constant deliberations of the map committee takes three tables and half the room; while a giddy hide-and-seek weaves to avoid their corralling parents.

Finally, all is ready. I hand out home-made rabbit ears and speak them forth. "Ride of the Valkyries" trumpets us out the doors, ears attached, as we head into the night.

Stealing up with lights off, amid snickering and whispers, stealthy volunteers slip across lawns to place an egg hunt and baskets on unsuspecting domiciles.

Poor kids will wake tomorrow to find the Easter Bunny really does exist.

Cars - 1

It was foggy rain. I was hugging the line, within safe margins to the triple "S" drop on Highway 1. Suddenly the front of a long, ocher-yellow Cadillac appeared cutting the right road-edge of my lane in the turn directly below. Starting a try to the left, my brakes locked swinging my van around sideways on the wet road. As his car came back across toward his side, and I was heading fully backwards, spinning around him on the right, I see his bulging wide-eyes staring up at me. The van kept spinning right around the back of his car, eucalyptus and asphalt swirling like dancers, and straightened perfectly back into my lane - on my way as if nothing had happened.

Cars and Youth - 2

Is youth dumb? I had a long Olds 88 with the big engine. 396 cubes. My friends called it the "Bob Sled" - I wasn't above going 100 or more on the long straight-a-ways. Zooom. Quite a car. It smoked bad and I would let the tires go until they had to be changed.

I pulled south and shot at 105 toward San Francisco. Along about Santa Rosa, I thought to myself "You know, I bet the tires are getting pretty bad about now."

I decided to head into a junk yard and see what kind of tires they had.

Pulling off, I came around the frontage and into the entrance. -Got out at the office and yelled over to the owner asking if he had any tires. As he opened his mouth, all four tires exploded like shotgun blasts and the car sank to the ground. There were gaping holes and exposed belts on all four baldies.

The owner's mouth just hung open.

––––––––––––––––––––––––––––

End of the Bob Sled - 3
(continued from previous)

The smoking got worse. I kept telling myself it didn't matter. If somebody else didn't like it, too bad. I went too fast for any attitude to catch me.

Heading north over the Golden Gate Bridge, I got snarled in traffic. Dead stopped, there came a multitude of jeering voices. Seven kids hung from the windows of the car to my left, all holding the their noses, laughing and yelling "EHWOOOooo!"

My defenses usurped utterly, I laughed and knew I had to do something about the car. It was a Norman Rockwell moment.

Artichoke

The empty, frozen December found me penniless in my empty, frozen house.

An old couple had passed in the summer, three roads off and left their large garden; - which had died away as well.

All except an artichoke plant that sat in the front, outside, along the fence.

I had seen it as I had been hungry - but I had a pauper's high, tony morals. It wasn't mine and I knew it.

Even though, - the flowers had been cut and taken, and all other vegetables had been harvested from the grounds; - they were the thieves. Purloined by the profligate scavengerhood.

Not me. But now the winter had fallen. The garden was long left. Frozen, flat rows of brown stubble and icy sticks.

Only the one, huge artichoke globe that had gone to seed. It spread open on its stem like an iron claw.

But it wasn't mine, - and I knew it.

No one had taken it and it was the largest artichoke I'd ever seen.

And I was hungry.

And it was Christmas.

I waited until the black of night, around nine o'clock and strode stridently over the frozen road and its naked ruts, stealthily through intervening properties. I wore my tattered plaid and Dojo Gi. I strode undetected and cut quickly, defensively embarrassed and muttering to myself about the ethics upon which I trespassed.

It made a marvelous and handsome Christmas Dinner, in my frozen house. In my frozen little town.

_____

The Cure

Once upon a time, in a small town, many miles away, there was a rollicking bash in the local bar. I can't remember if there was a band but the music was going and the people were going. I ran out of drink money but received many shots of wide and varying variety. As I normally don't drink, the next day was hung-over city. When I wandered past the bar, vague friends from the blurry before, entreated me in saying there was a hang-over cure everyone knew. I guess you had to be a bar insider to know about these things and being the early morning patrons, these four were staunch insiders.

I also remembered Rick Diran's story of a hang-over cure he'd received in an old Mexican bar - after a similar night in old Mexico.

He described it as a multiple layered, multiple colored affair in a tall, skinny glass. 'Said it cured him right up. These people's cure is a half beer chugged quickly. They assured me it worked perfectly every time.

Of course, when you hit it, it makes you instantly drunk again. - They all laughed. Hang-over cures are the joke every serious bar goer knows the minute some newbie is foolish enough to take the bait.

Don't forget this.

_____

Doctors

Don told me a story about his good friend, Rich McCovey.

The vet had told him his cat had leukemia and had to be put down. Rich didn't adhere to having the doc put his cat to sleep and said he'd take care of it privately.

He and a friend got a bottle of whiskey and took the cat, and their rifle, down to the river.

They had a drink or two and said their farewells to the cat, etc but found it was moving around too much. Wanting to be sure there was no pain and a perfectly humane procedure, they decided to bury the cat up to the neck - so it couldn't move so much.

At the same time, a family had begun setting up a picnic, some small distance away. Their ten year old daughter had popped over and observed the two armed men trying to bury the cat.

She ran back crying where-upon the Sheriff was called.

The Sheriff arrived, and although the two had progressed further into the bottle, Rich explained how the doctor had said the cat was terminal and how he loved the cat and how the best thing was for him to take care of it rather than the vet, and then also why they had decided to bury the cat before shooting it, etc.

The Sheriff said he understood entirely, every point and didn't charge them for the firearm in a public place nor animal abuse, etc, - just bundled them off with the DUI.

The cat... - lived another 10 ten years and died at 16.

Atomic Fire Ball Contest

The girls were four, five and six and challenged an Atomic Fire Ball contest.

The label on the candy decanter near the front register answered the "what are Atomic Fire Balls?" question.

Four round, red balls were purchased, divvied and popped. Their confident giggles declared victory; they KNEW who would lose the Atomic Fire Ball contest.

Ya ever eaten an Atomic Fire Ball?

Blackbird Sings on the Edge on Night...

Bob had new digs just off the long strip on the outskirts of Woodside; down from Portola Valley and a long abandoned lofty life. Such is fate. A small green thing with low ceilings. It was the black of night in the dead of winter and a certain squawk and cawing of bird conversations drifted from the back room. Slippery reflections swam in his eyes, "They're discussing you." Bob's smile sat in the dark under a mask of piercing curiosity, presented entirely as a prop for the play of the mysterious. Of course, my part is wondering what horrors await. All part of the performance. "They're deciding whether to kill you."
How will I know?
"Soon, one of them will come down and judge."
Sure enough, the clack of claws landing on old woodwork preceded a large Raven walking into the room and staring with his beak pushed straight in the air. I see his glimmering eye looking right at me. Presently he walked back and fluttered onto the crisscross dowels Bob had in the closet for their perch.
Bob sat back. "I guess you live..."

The Bonanza

You're walking down the city street, through a slow
stream of glum expressions, when some guy bounds past
with a side of beef yelling "Free at the Superdome!"

The crowd starts pushing and you're carried onward in
the common surge.

Gleeful people trundle cases of milk, bales of fresh coffee,
boxes of steak. Large-screen televisions, seemingly too
big to handle, weave through, - along with stereos and
designer furniture.

Halfway, a shared euphoria irresistibly breaks across
everyone's face and through the crowd: It's a Bonanza for
all!

Pushing through the crush, under the looming "Superdome Entrance", you find a madhouse of bustling activity as
everyone packs away goods from huge, open container-
cars sitting just inside.

You see, that's how it is with ants.

Econoline

I was young and had an old '62 Econoline van. A monstrous joke of mis-design, where the first of endless vexations to come was the leaky engine cover that makes occupants green sick on long trips.

So began the torturous procession of fits and non-starts, backfires and flame-outs that ruled my life for that time. One becomes expert at manipulating an ever changing subtlety of broken, jury-rigged, draped and taped electrical wiring.

Visiting my old neighborhood, miles from home, while wrestling pops and explosions, gnashing of teeth, and a last gasp, it finally ground me to the curb.

Got out and slammed the door as hard as I could, cussing. -Kicking the obdurate beast, punching the side.

It was getting twilight and after pacing, I jumped in to give it another try. The ensuing explosion set the whole engine afire.

That was IT! - I had absolutely had it and stalked off in a fume yelling the appropriate expletive at the top of my lungs.

Witnessing the scene from their offices across the street were the Superintendent of Schools and his janitor. They immediately ran across with their fire-extinguishers and met the inferno with an equally huge billowing blast of retardant foam.

I heard them entreating my return from down the street. I had gotten far enough away where their figures appeared about 1/4" tall.

I joined them and without a word, our attention turned toward the vehicle.

The whole interior was dripping with burnt, greenish black slime. Acrid smoke rose from the engine. The strands of wire had come apart and hung without insulation.

I pulled off my coat and swathed the sludge from the inside of the window. - Something from my deep, intimate knowledge just guided me. I stuck the key in, it turned right over and I left the astounded Superintendent and janitor watching as I drove off.

Barpool

I'd go play pool in Smiley's Bar, the only pool tables and the only bar in our sleepy little coastal town.
It was a sunny Saturday and there were 150 gleaming Harley's pulled up, all leaning on their stands with their front wheels facing left.
The little 40x40 barroom was packed to the gills. My quarter came up.
I was a guitar player and had the habit of whistling a lead over every tune from the jukebox. Some people find that annoying but I just have a good time.
I played for a hour or so and when I left the bar, a local with a very agitated expression grabbed me off to the side and said: "Man, did you see what happened in there? - Three bikers were in each other's face, the whole place was about to explode when you started playing. And then your whistling just made everybody back off and start drinking their beers and enjoying themselves. You saved the whole town! - Didn't you see?"

Birdsong

This beauty, the lush green of the glade

The gentle dance of birdsong drifting in the air

This is how it was when they first ventured here, before
the army's drudge broke the silence, before the earth
was ground under their passing.

When the Legions spearheaded north
When their scouts first passed through

This is how it was for the knights and serfs
The Axis and the Allies
    the pursuers and pursued

This is how it was
after they left

Nature's soft poem
       to dispel their departure

The lush of the glade

the birdsong

Burlingame

I wasn't even in high-school yet and was already running with the wrong crowd.

The Nishimoto brothers and the guys who hung with them. From 19th Avenue. I was beginning my rebellion from a sedate upper middle-class background.

San Mateo and Burlingame high-schools are the famous rivals. Thanksgiving always ends the football season with the Little-Big Game. This contrasts the "Big Game" between Stanford and Cal.

Alumni come from all over the country.

The regular season is a lead-up, festooned with night-games.

These are the magical promise of a garden of experiences to come.

I rode with my parents in the family station-wagon. Through the black silhouettes, the pounding energy thunders in the dark; and blazing lights ignite the sky.

Not betraying my true motivations, I vow to return after the game.

But I am a rebel. I do not plan to see this spectacle. I have a set of purloined car-keys and my friends await near the "Hasty-Tasty" hamburger stand.

My parents find parking inside the row of eucalyptus that line the train track just across from the park.

It is not long before my friends and I are joy-riding up and down the San Francisco Peninsula. I can no longer remember our adventures but when we arrived back in the late forth-quarter, we are aghast to find someone had parked in the empty spot.

We drove back and forth as the winning goal exploded from the stadium.

The emergency pressing, everyone jumped out, surrounded the offending Impala and, by arm-strength alone, carried it out.
Quickly reversing our long Plymouth, we shut the doors just as my parents approached. My friends became autonoms and disappeared in slow-motion.

My parents never knew.

————————————————————————

Once Upon a Time

She was of the untouchable class. Dressed in the sharpest
- from London or Paris, or maybe New York. Such fashion
is the private life of the elevated world; and she was with
the elevated group. The big international dealer, Jose
from Chile and his group.

This girl was petite and new to their company.

Jose's girl-friend was a majestic being. A shining beauty
with an open expression as big as the sky. She could
humble evil with a glance and had proved so according to
a story I had heard.
These were the beautiful people. He had a yacht and several homes. I was only remotely connected by music and
proximity in this small town but otherwise, miles away.

Driving down the Overlook, two or three weeks later, I
saw a couple wrapped around each other and barely able
to walk for their fumbling. It was Jose and this new one. I
smiled for the adventure and good time they were having.

It may have become spring, I showered and headed
downtown in my colorful van, long hair flowing.
I pulled into the parking near the community-center.
There was a small, pixy-like creature crouched in a darkened staircase across the street whom I noticed suddenly
shooting, with swept-back wings in a wide arc on a target-
path that would intersect directly - with me.
Landing low and infront like bat-woman she stared wide-
eyed. Making up her mind, judging. I carefully ventured
"What are you on?" To which she popped erect, twisting
back and forth like a child and biting her finger with a

giggle, " ...Life"

She was on acid.

She was certainly beautiful but I knew I needed to help her find her way back to wherever she had been. I was asking where she belonged and she was imploring that we run off and make love.

She was snuggling in, kissing my chest, I was querying for the house I should take her when I realized this was HER. This is the little one from Jose's group.

It may be that Jose is wondering, possibly at this very moment, where she fell off to. This is an even greater reason to be sure she finds her way home. It's nice she finds me attractive while on acid, but I don't need my motivations questioned by anyone; - let alone Jose. Let alone a possibly bereaved Jose.

To her objections I brought her back across the street and deposited her to the appropriate doorstep.

Next day, I again shower and head downtown. And again I pull into the community-center parking. I intend playing guitar in the empty room.

As I pull out my case, she is right there. She explains she is no longer on acid and that she had been upset that it had prevented a proper meeting. She said she'd waited all night for the acid to get out of her system.

I took her inside so I could practice - but really to show off my guitar skills.

However, she did not care about my guitar nor guitar playing - at all. This was easily discerned after four or five seconds. So we packed up and went out to the cliffs.

This is a female who lives for love. No so chosen male is allowed more than the fumbling, wrapped misdirection I had seen on Overlook.

We head back to my van and it is quickly unavoidable. I start pulling my boots off; probably because of the van, she says "Right now?" I say "Right now" - and we proceed on a three and half hour window-steamer.

We talked about an adventurous escape across the country in my colorful van but of course, life will take her on to new horizons very soon.

I saw her some months later. I was at the beach and heard her "Ew-ww" (- a particular love call) from the high sea-wall. She ran along the down-slope and I up the sand from below. When we were ten feet apart, she slid off the edge -never doubting a lover's protection- and into my arms.

Such a life was she.

Cash Dock
A sweet, little ol' lady with all white hair asked for help with her first try at the super-market self-check stand. The service gal told her she was next while she helped me tap in a bakery item. My machine froze, and then spit the wrong change out across the floor in a stream. Everyone helped pick it up and the service-gal used her calculator to count. She opened the machine housing for the correct change when the coin box flipped over, spilling its contents. The elderly woman stood with aghast expression, to which I bellowed: "Well, Good Luck!" We both roared with laughter. -One of those great moments.

Don was a youth. In a new world of youths. Tall, curly hair.

Don's traveling circus would marvel colleges, large and small across the country.
Making a grand, Barnum-style impact in the middle of campus, his crew would setup a huge "Geodesic Dome" as their tent. Don had cleverly obtained proper license from the famous Buckminister Fuller which insured their free welcome wherever they went.

Jugglers on monocycles and magic tricks would cast their spell to dazzle the curious of all ages; and for Don, especially the girls.

They delighted a constant stream of students and on-lookers with their colorful play and entertainments.

The big lesson for Don's life came when they ran out of money in the mid-west.

Here, Don was responsible for his crew and his people. Going broke was also a complete violation of the stern stricture of his father's precept.

This was stinging embarrassment. His people were soon to be hungry; and he found himself hearing only a blank echo with this small town for a back-drop.
He didn't even know where they were - nor how they got there.

Then the town cop showed up. He handed Don a small piece of paper and drove off.
It said, "the mayor wants to see you."

Entering a calm, staid office, the mayor surprised by offering lunch. Keeping a straight face, Don listened to the tedious concerns of town life and politics.

After a time, the mayor swung his chair around to open a cabinet, wherein a large variety of secreted magic tricks lay hidden. Most of these were from "The Magic Castle." A turret and stone edifice in Hollywood where all the world's top magicians are registered and which is considered the Mecca and epitome of Magic for all it's practitioners, world-wide. -A place Don knew well.

The Mayor explained that he and the City Council leader and the Chief of Police were magicians and they too had found themselves alone and broke in this town some fifteen years before.

As magic is the practice of illusion, they had made themselves look like a mayor, a council leader and a police chief and had simply placed themselves at the head of the town's institutions.
He went on to explain that this town had provided a good life and when seeing Don, their group decided it was perhaps a sign for their convenient retirement.
If Don would say the magic words: "I will", Don could have the town.

Just say the magic words...

Unfortunately for them, Don went back to college and learned to handle money.

Yoshi - 1
Yoshi had first come over to go to college. He didn't speak any English at the time and when he decided where he'd go, he just put his finger on the map. Wanting to see the real U.S.A., he pointed into the center of the country - Paris Texas.
He flew in, drove to town, pulled over and fell asleep. When he awoke, his car was directly before a strange store front. Within, he used his electronic translator to inquire for a rental - which he found upstairs.
It took a couple months to understand what the large KKK above the door meant.

Maybe he became invisible and they couldn't see him. He lived there two years.

———————————————————

Yoshi - 2
Yoshi went across the border for a day. On his way back, the Immigration Officers said he was a "wet-back" and his passport was fake. They confiscated his papers.
So Yoshi found himself traveling through Mexico. He said it was ok because he saw new places and the Mexican girls liked him just fine.

———————————————————

Lawn
We knew they were there when they went on food sortes. Little eyes would poke-up - several at a time. Suddenly, one would skidder out and disappear under the house.
                We knew then, - the game was afoot.

Moth

There was to be a "play in the round" performed on the open floor, with an encircling audience in chairs and recliners forming the perimeter.

In the bustling set-up, I was repairing a microphone in a dressing-room. As the pre-show energy built, someone opened a bottle of red wine. Those present sipped as preparations continued.

With less than half a glass consumed, Moth began a joy-ful observance, from where suddenly her legs collapsed and she crumpled to the floor; appearing altogether totally inebriated.

Her boyfriend, Bear wrested her up explaining she was allergic to alcohol and helped her into the auditorium. From their perch, her eyes appeared like those of a par-rot pushed high up into the bridge of her nose and sup-porting her sagging countenance like two nails holding an old coat.

Soon the play began and quickly proceeded to visceral drama, with players arguing in a charged portrayal of elder and younger members of a family.

Suddenly Moth had had enough from the family no-account and sprang to the floor, punching the guy: "You can't say that to HER!"

Fitting right in, most thought it was part of the play. Next morning, she received the highest and most favorable reviews.

JP

JP is a big man. Long beard. A working man. Broad suspenders hold low-slung pants.

JP is heading out of the convenience store with a 16oz cola when he sees two hunters pull in next to him with a huge buck spread out across their hood. Its swollen tongue sticks out under two crossed eyes.

Two steps more and JP has a stroke - which throws a instantly chaotic topsy-turvy into the newly reeling scene. He stumbles forward holding the coke and falling head over chest onto the hood-ornament. His left side frozen, his body teetering to fall, busted skull or broken-neck onto a concrete abutment beckoning just below. The clasped coke is his only balancing offset.

Slowly his body drapes around and slumps over the hood. He can't quite tell the difference between himself and the deer, both staring in the reverse reflection of the convenience-store window. But he was the one with a beard.

Suddenly, feeling begins to return to part of his left side and he pushes himself away from the brink, and certain deathly fall, and notices he hasn't spilled the coke.

Pushing himself upright against the windshield, he was sure glad to have a nice icy Coke.

Not a guy to bother with doctors, he headed back to work.

JP2

Also called Johnny Reb; - talks about electric fences: At 13, he and his little buddy were out in the hills. Short-cutting back through the cow pasture, his friend went to the post to take a leak. Johnny told him it was "hot" but the kid didn't believe him. He was pissin' on the post and Johnny watched the stream slowly head closer and closer to the wire. Knocked him straight down.
That kid couldn't piss for a week.
Johnny Reb: "I told 'em!"

———————————————————

Last Laugh on God

Practice breathing. You can do this by meditation, weight-training, martial arts or yoga. Get good at it. Then, at the end of your life when you've drawn your last breath, you can stop and take another. You'll see God do a double-take and you can snicker.

———————————————————

Duck

Another rocket had gone off from Vandenberg. I swung down into the Duxbury Reef parking lot and climbed the cliff.
There was a duck standing there on one foot. I sat down next him and we watched together.
The first stage cut off and six plumes from explosive bolts marked the separation. The second stage ignited and proceeded away while the late sun painted white light into an expanding six-peddle blossom that slowly filled the whole sky.
We watched for 45 minutes or so.

Crew Boss

The Crew Boss liked to run his people like a military camp, holding regular morning meetings before punching in, and on regular activities that everyone otherwise regularly knew perfectly well.

He would then march his crew onto the elevator for the forth floor, with the boss always emerging first, and the crew to follow him off.

Dick would reach under his arm and tap the third floor button - whereupon, the boss would stride forth, the elevator doors closing behind him.

He would come charging onto the forth floor, red faced and flustered; but he never knew who did it and could never see it coming.

Crew Boss2: Office

The Crew Boss had a hearing-aid. Dick and the other people used to go up to him and start talking in the following fashion: "Rup- yip - stup - yep - zert - -phit- " - to which he would yank the hearing-aid off and hang it from his lamp, muttering.

The Crew Boss put up with his bad hearing aid for years.

Bolinas

They had a contingent of jazz musicians - top players. A couple of the guys had been in Downbeat - and were rising stars of note. There were several Beat-era poets. Bolinas had been the San Francisco beat poets enclave outside the city.

They had a thing they called "The Ritual" every Sunday - where whoever was around would come over to do the 'Ritual' free jazz jam - with poet Max Crosley doing voice over. Usually about five or so people blasting away.

Once, they said there'd be a special New Years Eve jam. I went over - several drummers had showed up but Steven Josel was the always resident man - and better than any other trap players - so I don't remember how many others were playing. There were five guitar players - but as every horn player knows, almost no guitar player can really play. I plugged into a Twin Amp that was there. There was a grand piano - and, I believe, Pablo Picasso's niece on Cello. Even though they all could have top gigs any where in the world, they had flown in from Paris and Tokyo, Germany and London. There were 43 horn players.

At about 10 minutes to 12, I started in and Josel was right under me. The others started; -and while I may have been the fastest guitar player in the world at the time, and playing fantastic music, etc- none the less, by the time midnight struck, I was being dragged from long dangling reins, through the dust and detritus, of a nitro-fuel rocket-ride free-jazz stage-coach tearing open the very fabric of time and space. I remember seeing a three column double contra-bass clarinet gyrating next to guy playing a piccolo-saxophone.

- You'd a loved it.

Contrasts
I remember turning to see a long, lanky red wolf in a powder-blue harness tied to a bike rack, stoic against the breezy bustle of a Sausalito afternoon.

The Bully
Tim's mother is Japanese, father caucasian and Tim could easily be taken for dark Irish. Tim's cousin, Jimmy was a whole blood Japanese who had a ZERO tolerance for prejudice.
Kurt, the school bully, would always have things to say and actions to take that were constantly less than peers or parents may have hoped.

Kurt was never fun.

One lunch time, Tim leans over to Kurt and says, "Call him a Jap -"
Kurt looks down the tables toward Jimmy and says, "Jap."
Tim can see Jimmy's ears twist and start to turn red. Tim whispers to Kurt, "He didn't hear ya"; where a snickering Kurt then augments another, "Jap"
Jimmy's body launched into the air like a re-coiling leaf-spring and came down with all fists and feet.

The pounding lasted for a very brief few seconds before Jimmy walked off and Kurt looked like an accordion.

To this Tim immediately chimed: "I meant, 'Don't call him a Jap, don't call him a Jap!'"

Eternal Life
A sleeping man perceived that eternal life might be attained, in experiment, by the temporary conjoining of his neural-net mind within the lattice of a static DNA architecture, as might be found in some beetles and spiders.
Oddly, such transmugration became fetchingly possible that very moment when, as he rose through the dream-state, a small house-spider happened onto direct contact with his eye.
Unfortunately, as he rolled over, the spider became crushed under his body.
Still perfectly conscious, and seeming no more remarkable than a dried out daddy long-legs, he was shaken off the blankets and onto the rug when his friends cleaned out the house.

What really Happens after you Die
You wake up in traffic behind someone going 3 1/2 miles an hour SLOWER than you.

How many artists are acknowledged in their own time?
None, people are too cheap to elevate a breathing human - besides, they have to be told someone was good by others.
Otherwise, THEY'D be a great artist.
But if they were a great artist, they'd be too broke to buy their own stuff.

Einstein
It was a storming, black night and Einstein was dying.
At about 3:30 am he suddenly looked up to the attend-
ing nurse and began to speak. His finishing words trailed
off in his last breath.
Later, the reporters hung on every word of her descrip-
tion of the last moments of Albert Einstein's life. When
she stopped, they asked what were the last words of the
great man?

She: "How do I know, I don't speak German."

Friday Night in America
Skip was back on leave from the Marines and we all
crowded into the steel-guitar player's perfectly-restored
black '52 Ford. Some girls were spotted. They rocketed
away, we gave chase. An hour plus chase.
Up to the new subdivision, squealing through the High-
lands, back down into Burlingame, out along Peninsula
Ave, into San Mateo, over and around and through the
Hillsdale shopping mall and out into Belmont, across and
down and rippling through the bendy cul-de-sacs, until
they finally hung the wrong right to a downhill dead-
end.
Their car sat in settling dust as we slid up along side. The
window rolled down and sweetest face said, "You know,
we're really not worth it."
To which Skip, in his Marine uniform and best smiling
movie-star expression replied, "Yes, it was fun" -
And we all cruised happily on to the next adventure.

Knowing

You're over at your DJ friend's, who has you tap out
rhythms on the mixer. You find you can get funny little rip-
ples and slurs in the notes as you play and decide you are
going to be the ballsiest, new Pop King on the Scene and
hit it big. - You see the future perfectly and go right ahead
and plan your new life. You get sequined shirts and slick
hair and new friends. In a music store you bump into an
old blues man playing harmonica, who you quickly forget.
On tour, a year and a half later, you get a flat tire in a small
back-water. You come to a cross-roads where a lean man
in black top-hat asks if you need assistance. Obliging, he
drops you by a tavern and you find yourself playing a nasty
slide guitar with people drinking wine and smoking reefer.
You forget your former life because this is real, get-down
music and these are real, get-down people and, of course,
they're drinking wine and smoking reefer.

Another year and a half passes when a princess appears,
breathing African secrets in your ear but you notice her
words have the familiar rippling slur that now trademarks
your new fame. The rhythmic slurring seems to echo from
the opposite side of your skull and slithers into a whole
separate sentence: "What happened to the Pop King?"
To which you reply,   "Old dogs learn new tricks... "

---

100 Gibson Guitar Theory

If you have 100 Gibson Guitars (of the same model),
THREE are good.
The rest are pedestrian at best, some are bad. They just
didn't glue together right. They fight the notes. Something's wrong.
3 out of 100.
You can apply this to people, wines, hotels and restau-
rants, cars. You name it.
Three are good.

No. 23

Scrolling 19th century pictures on the internet, the final one is empty. The forward button returns the same non picture for higher numbers proceeding beyond the index.

After a few clicks an old image presents, but a familiar face. Someone alive in the 1860s, who you have known. You know you have known her.

It is the past but it could be the future. It is simply not now. But you know her. You know you know her.

Diny

Queuing the checkout, someone's mother was looking to load groceries from their cart while watching her purse and keeping her three year old in tow.
Just behind, I noticed a tray full of plastic Dinosaurs on the rack to my left. Her little one was eying the wonders of the candy spread from her feet to above her head.
I signaled the cashier that I was paying and took a red Diny down to peek around my left leg. She noticed the Diny, as it was making Diny movements and reached up instinctively to take it. This new addition was immediately hers and she knew it unquestioningly.
Only the cashier saw.

New for 1958 - The Atomic Driveway

It had radioactive material mixed in the concrete. Melted the snow. Kept the driveway clear. It was great! 'cept the warm surface attracted all the neighborhood dogs who found it a great place to leave their piles.

Careful What You Wish For

His grandfather had used the '51 Studebaker Pickup for the shop truck before Kyle got it. Added to his collection of always rusting Americana, Kyle keeps them up as best he can. He and uncle Glenn took over the family auto-motive service and fix anything thrown at them.

Kyle can get short fused in the daily grind, as Glenn can testify, when car-parts don't act right. And they don't act right a lot.

It was a long day and Kyle had been put to the test. Car after car battled Kyle's sensibilities and his fuse had been burnt out four or five times when finally "closing" prom-ised a quiet moment to get the 'Studie' tweaked for the weekend.

When he rolled it around front, the clutch blew out for the final straw.
Glenn looked over when Kyle jumped out, yelling to the Heavens: "Just tell me, what could -possibly- HAPPEN NEXT!?"

To which, a soaring seagull immediately answered with a huge dollop directly across Kyle's forehead and nose.

Glenn fell to the ground laughing. -By far, his best day in the automobile business!

Sidecar

Glenn's dad took in a Harley with a side-car. -Told 16 year old Glenn to keep his hands off.

It sat facing the road at the end of the used car line where Glenn had to shine it up, along with the other cars. It sure looked pretty. It had shiny dials and out-stretched handlebars.

His dad took off for the parts-house and told Glenn to "leave that bike alone."

But somehow Glenn got on the seat. - An' somehow, the engine got started.

When he pulled the handlebars around, the bike took it as an excuse for the big get-a-way and took Glenn off at full throttle. The bike and Glenn argued for control but what can sixteen year old do against a full grown Harley? They spun out of control in the yard next door before Glenn launched into air over the lumber pile. -Got caught up in the neighbor's clothes line, but the Harley mowed it over ok, and the two of them finally settled out back at the line where they started.

Just a little worse for the wear.

Marriage

At the end of his life, Snarlin Harlin told his wife, Leotta to flush his ashes down the toilet.

-She didn't do that, either.

Tahoe

I guess I was about eight. My mom had rented a long Cris-Craft speedboat to take us boys board skiing.

At some point we wiped out and paddled about while she swung around. The ski-board was nowhere to be seen.

Then we see the rope being tightly pulled back and forth from below, like some huge fish had it.

Pollywogging, we watched for the first inexorable signs from the slow climb beneath us.

Soon, the tombstone-shaped, greenish board came shooting from the left, about 20 feet down, to disappear to the right. Then, swoosh, 15 feet from the right to the left. Back and forth, almost too fast to see.

It was probably cutting through the water at about 20 miles an hour. Knifing up closer to our wiggling bodies, pass by pass.

No worries, it finally popped up - and we continued the day.

Mail Box

My ex had a nutty sister who got credit cards in the mail. She'd max them out at the mall. Since that meant she was a buyer, the banks kept sending more cards - which she'd go max out. Finally the sheriff came, charged her and took the cards, but the banks kept sending more cards which she'd keep maxing out. They put her on probation but she couldn't stop. It went on years. She's still getting cards in the mail.

She loved going to the mall.

Color
Some animals - like budgie birds, - and a lot of insects,
see whole ranges of color we don't.
That's why they have such shimmering color in their
feathers and bodies, etc.
A big part of the budgie's lives is mating - they appear to
each other like bejeweled Princes and Princesses. Glimmering, resplendent.

---

x-dreame
Woman comes in and out of one's life. She's here and
does things. Sometimes it's wholly benign but we know
she's capable of stirring up trouble. You see she secrets a
garage-door clicker and have become suspicious that she
clicks herself over to Hades. -Stirs stuff up over there.
Then you notice she doesn't seem to age.
You start thinking about getting your hands on the
clicker. Maybe trick her into clicking it when she doesn't
know - so she's gone without taking it with her.
Maybe you start having the clicker.

Rock and Roll Breakfast with Bob and Ned
What happened that I looked around? -no more than
a second. I remember their toothy smiles as their forks
withdrew from my plate, along with most of the meal.

Travis

My best friend had just returned from the Airforce with a new group of buddies, all stationed at Travis and all ready for good times and rolling weekends in the Bay Area.

Driving back at 3:30am, Decker had me come on base for breakfast. I was told to sign in using a certain number of digits.

There was a single line of guys in the middle of a huge, echoing aircraft hanger, all queuing for a lonely 2 x 2 desk manned by a single Sergeant. Each guy was signing in while slipping somebody's service card around behind him for the next guy.

I took the card from the guy in front, presented it to the Sergeant, scribbled the digits and a signature, and slipped the card around where it resumed play.

Another single line in constant motion passed by the food grill, where the cook asked how I liked 'em. "Runny yokes and no snot," whereupon my two eggs were tossed on the grill, knifed in half, turned once and delivered to my held-forth plate.

Best eggs I ever had.

Cats & Skunks

Did you know: Cats and skunks get along. They play at night.

Playland at the Beach had one of those large spinning, wooden saucers onto which everyone would jam themselves waiting for the start. A human operator ran it and wrangled the kids.

Slowly, at first, the unfortunate outsiders and little ones were spun off to the padded perimeter.

The remaining squeezers then got the faster and faster treatment until the final fast spin revealed the conquering victor.

You could do it all day. But you needed more tickets.

Riders

Dominik was Basque. He had rosy cheeks and thin, almost purple lips. He loved his Harley.

He was on acid, rocketing at over 100 mph through the dry hills. Caressing the tank, he was one with every nudge and nuance of the muscular race horse running inside its vibrating block. The ticking beat of its heart and he in time with it.

Another biker came up from the desert below - screaming over the near ridge. They raced at each other. Turn and return, jumping the space between them.

Burning through spitting sand, they started circling on a flat clearing. Closer and closer - at 75 miles an hour. Tighter and tighter - until they reached out and clasped hands. Spinning and howling in a blaze of wild glory...

The Best

The best rider Vard ever saw besides himself, -was a cop.
CHP guy.

He picked him up somewhere on the Peninsula. Vard ran.
Vard was naturally good at everything he did. Bikes, -
small criminal enterprises, burglaring, dope dealing,
roust-abouting. Heavy equipment operator. He knew how
things worked, was the best at what he did and collected
many friends and associates around him. Naturally charismatic, naturally good looking. He had a quick wit, easy
way and he always had something going on. He was wild
and everybody liked him.

So naturally, he wasn't going to get ticketed by some CHP
guy.

But the CHP guy held on. Vard started him through the
town. They chased down alleyways, through fences and
backyards and over the hillsides, jumping ravines. Out to
the quarry and down the impossible drop. Vard, "He went
down it!" Under the freeway, through the old Bayside
subdivision and finally into the sparse weeds along the
slew. The cop thought he had him.

There was a tie-cable that held a large drainage pipe
suspended over the waterway. Vard ran across it. The
fat wheels on the CHP Harley were incapable of the two
inch width so the two rolled up and looked at each other
across the water. Both waved. Both knew.

Phoenix and the Dragon

The Phoenix flies over the water. Myriad brilliant stars
blink from its surface.

He sails lazily over the waves,
  their mirrored reflections ignite his shimmering form.

Feigning unawareness;
  - his shadow runs after him. Trying to keep up. Scurrying
like a badger.

In the deep is the Dragon...

The Dragon is curious.

The Dragon knows it's the Phoenix, but the Dragon can't
help himself. Curiosity is the SUKI of the Dragon.

The Dragon is transfixed
        ...maybe it's not the Phoenix...

The shadow moves hypnotically. It's silence is thunder as
it roars across the rippling veil above.

Curiosity unbearable, the Dragon rises up
for that dark form - fluttering across his eyes.   -just across
the curtain...

  and as he reaches out...

   The Phoenix grabs him up!

Bird Ship

There's a San Francisco ship in the Mothball Fleet that the birds have taken over. It's their ship. They occupy all decks. Birds in different countries know about it. They come visit on their way up North and others on their way South. Locals live there year round.

Humans keep trying to move it now and then. Over here, over there; - but the birds go with it. They don't care about other ships, just this ship.

It's theirs.

Meeting of a Shaman

I need to ask you - I had a dream.

I was a musician and knew blacks - - but I had a dream. It was at a place - like a college but not a new place - and a place where people were. Busy at their concerns - moving and talking. Bothered about each other; normal interests.

I saw a girl. I knew her name. I can see her now. She carried something under her dress. It carried all the souls of black people - waiting to return. Attached to her. It had a name.

She was joyous - she'd tell you about it but you had to ask. I can see it. It had shiny, worn nut-shell around the end with woody rope-like husk and hair around the outside. It wasn't dry and it wasn't wet. It held the multitude, which you could only catch faint glimpse.

What was it's name? I can see it, I was shown it and I see her. I told someone who barely caught my words.

What was it's name? Caba shena - ? Something . I need to ask you.

Afternoon

Climb above the grinding chaos of the valleys, into the
high reaches - to the frail meditations of a skinny, ancient priest. His gaze sits serenely on the far, flat horizon.
The hot afternoon bears silently in and a single bird
soars. Motioning downward, we fall to the forests below.
Monkeys race through the canopy while huge serpents
churn beneath. A howling tiger guards his temple ram-
parts, under the first clear stars to pierce the blue above.

But we must return - before the twilight descends.

First Heat

It's 98 degrees when I step outside and see a snow white
butterfly flitting into the sun from under the shadows. It
flickers closer then further but seems to prefer the sun.
It's all alone and makes its way down the building to
disappear in the wind.
Where's it going?

The Shunned

His dark jaundiced skin hung like moldy paper. The
sunken eyes stared from his gaunt face. A large, tar-
nished belt-buckle strapped the loose pants - from falling
off his overly tall and sagging frame. A frightening and
shunned figure. I engaged him on the road in the dark
of midnight. He said they had removed his pituitary. We
talked about hidden worlds and the inner secrets of the
larger universe.
He was - a wonderful man.

Dave Packard

My father was an early friend of Dave Packard. He had the electronics shop in his garage. My dad handled his advertising, and they were hunting buddies.

Dave was a leader in all things. He marshaled his departments and projects throughout his career like a great general. A masterful controller in whom all placed unquestioned confidence.

He knew everyone and everyone loved him. He was a man's man.

They were on a deer hunt. About 15 huddled in the snowy road over Dave's direction at first light. On the other side of a berm stretched a long valley and Dave was instructing who should be where so all would have an even go at the game and everyone would be safe. Holding steady focus on the game-plan, Dave unbuckled his pants and took a crap right there without skipping a word. He stood back up, gently flicking snow to cover it with the edge of his boot. He finished his talk and they all went hunting.

The Return

Fanny, the fish-wife looks up to see a mossy, black barque hunkered in the pitching, brackish waves. Huge black knots arise from deeply furrowed crevasses, streaking the ancient timbers. It's held from the lacy lapping by a constant kneading drumbeat of endless frothy fingers; the whole ocean heaving it forward, to the long awaiting shore. Angry wind whips through feathery lichens to shake their slippery shadows across the bleached and weary bones - of our five ancient warriors, still clasping at their swords.

Facing the Sea

Rick and I would race straight off the 100 foot ocean cliffs
in Bolinas, jumping as big and far as we could stretch.
Nearly straight down, we knew we'd hit the detritus field
and allow 10 mighty strides to the bottom.
We did it all the time.

Later, I talked Danny the Drummer into trying. I jumped
down and skied 30 feet or so, entreating him to go for it.
There was a huge, untouched field waiting to take him,
ten feet to his side.
He finally let go of his misgivings and jumped. Unfortunately, the "field" was actually a slick rock-face with some
gravel on it.
With fierce and unflinching determination, ~and no
choice~ he rocketed, Wiley-coyote to his fate. Ponytail
blown straight back, he disappeared into a funnel of dust
and ground face first into the sand below. We all busted a
gut.
I don't know how he survived - but he climbed out of his
clean body impression and all was well. -Or at least, he
didn't look too different.

Stormy Mountain Night

Just naked, howling trees and wet pavement. Rounding
the sharp curve, a thirty foot rock occupies the entire
road. It has just dropped, no bounce. I steer straight
around on the cliff-edge without slowing. It disappears in
the eerie dark behind...

The Knight

You're out in the fields, that run along the forest. Your dog runs in after a rabbit. You go chasing. The forest is dense. You hear the dog up ahead.

You come by the edge of an old creek-bed. You slide down slightly but grab a branch and swing up to stay along the top of the old bank. The greens are lighter with the sun streaming through. The sandy gravel leads into a sweet glade where you find a hidden cave. You have the fantasy notion that there may be something in the cave, something waiting for you. Sure enough, you find ancient armor. You know about the legend of the great knight who saved the nation - but this is just wild coincidence. Still, it's strange, there has been injustice in the cities.

You take the armor out to your cart and head for home around the valley way. Feeling the lightness of the moment, you put the armor on and suddenly feel like maybe you could do something. Something to confront the ills of the world.- Maybe you could go forth, when called upon, and triumph. To exceed danger and do right, vanquishing wrongs. Set evil aside and become victorious. Somehow you know if you rode straight to the cave, the path would be open but no army could find it. It is a secret abode. As you pass, there are loud voices from town and a muffled scream.

One Day

Dusty hallway has old, dusty burglar alarm in high corner. An old janitor bumbles back and forth between rooms, moving his mops. A light blinks on the device and a laser zaps the cleaner who falls limp. A quiet buzzer starts an intermittent squeaking. Soon a vehicle rolls up outside and two robots make their way into the hall. Robot: "That's a shame. Was that the last of the humans?"

The Coondog

Coondog's quarter is up. We explain that the table has gone to 15-1 Ball, "Straight Pool", not 8-Ball, the fast bar-table thing he is used to.

We tell him it was the choice of the winner to change games. This is slow, deliberate, careful play. For instance, the 1 ball has to go to one of the side pockets, and the 15 ball has to go to the opposite side pocket, does he get that?

It's Coondog's turn and he'll play anyway.

So Coondog watches as I set the first careful, safe-shot, driving the outside balls gently to the rail and back - leaving the pack bunched in the center where they started. Coondog swigs his beer and slams the bottle down, gets up for his normal harddriving 8-Ball break-shot which makes us all wince.

He lays into it and the balls leave the table, blasted into an airborne jumble. A couple of balls hit the light. The 1 and the 15 strike each other, two-and-a-half feet above the table, and take a swan drive into the two side pockets. Coondog finishes the game out and changes it back to 8-Ball.

Mates

We were looking at Yogurts. I picked one out and perused the ingredients while she had drifted slightly to the right - for milk. Setting it back, I reached for her waist, while she reached for me, looking at the products. And as we touched, we saw we were reaching for mates that were now lost. A stranger, she was well-dressed, attractive and we both saw that we'd make a very perfect couple; - but laughed at this otherwise perfectly timed surprise.

Culture

I realize I'll probably not get to convince the Jews to become Gentiles.

You react, "that's impossible"

But why not? - After all, the gentiles are but peoples without a culture, right?

I mean, really - what culture do gentiles have?

And certainly the Jews would ask.

They have culture; long and rich culture. They've carted it with them over all these years.

The Gypsies have culture. India has culture. The Natives of the Americas have many, varied cultures.

And of course, the Arabic peoples.

And Japan, Japan is like the Jews with their closed culture. They are family. They know who they are; and everybody else are outsiders. "Gaijin" The Jews lament they "don't belong" - but really it's the outsiders that don't belong.

Gentiles. They were always an expansive bunch. Ready to move, ready to marry. Ready Freddy. Maybe it's the Neanderthal DNA. Always the outsiders.

So it's a question of culture. What's it good for? More pain than gain? Ask yourself.

(Of course, a Samurai determined at Seppuku isn't going to ask himself if he should have been an astronaut)

Portola Valley

Bob referred to his mother as, 'The Dragon' - she'd
laugh. But they had roaring squabbles.

She had the north side of the house, he had the rest.

We had a rock and roll band. $15. a week bought each
of us two meals and board. His mother was a great cook
and gourmand, so the meals were good.

The front had floor-to-ceiling picture windows which
swept across the whole home. It had seen a rich and
glorious life, twenty years gone.

They had had racing horses and knew movie stars. Lew
Costello had wanted to adopt Bob. But that was all in the
long-ago past.

We all sat around a lazy sunny Saturday watching 30s
reruns on their old black and white portable, propped on
an end-table. The Dragon came and went.

As the Dragon happened past, a scratchy version of
"We're in the Money" sputtered from the old TV - to
which, both Bob and the Dragon instantly jumped into
giddy song, - arms locked and swinging round and round
in a sudden riotous carousel mime, their index fingers
bobbing up and down in unison - "We're in the money -
we're in the money" switch directions, round and round
the other way "We're in the money - "

Date Palms

Long ago, date trees were surprised when humans kept
eating their seed which, of course, the dates had carefully designed to either kill animals outright or give them
the runs they'd never forget. Still, the little monkeys
didn't destroy the tress, so they shrugged it off. After all,
if humans are that stupid, well ...more power to them.

Philo Farnsworth. Inventor

His dad invented television. My dad, and Dave Packard, and their wives, the two Lucilles, watched Philo Sr turn the first television on, for the first time - on Green St in San Francisco.

Years later, I was friend of Philo Jr. He had invented the submarine engine with no moving parts. When he worked at Westinghouse. He never gave it to them.

He was a stocky build with a twinkle in sharp eyes.

He showed us a little plant, the size of a pea, consisting entirely of a single, heart-shaped leaf. "Take it home" What is it? - "It's called 'Mother of a Thousand Babies' - don't know why -"

It was cute. He said, "Looks cute, huh -"

We took it home and put it in a small pot by the window. Little heart-shaped leaflets started to appear along the heart-shaped rim. It began to look like something from Alice in Wonderland. It was even more cute!

I think we went to my parents house for a couple days. When we got back, Mothers of the Thousands of babies were growing from the shelves, the carpets, the books, the bedding, the window stiles. Along the floor in the bathroom. On the stairs.

I phoned up Philo but his laughter doffed my complaint before I could start. He said, "something wrong?"

Cute.

Roommates

A friend told me he came back to his apartment to find the shower-stall filled to the top with toilet paper. The roommate said he got it on sale.

The Way In -   [Hollywood1]

Don has a friend named Richard whose space-station novel and plot got into print and the movies. It remained on the Best Seller list in various countries for years. Versions of his design for a permanent space living utopia still appear in big blockbusters.

Richard describes his Hollywood experience:

Arriving for his pitch conference, the producer sat behind his large desk with his right-hand man, stoically behind.

Richard surmised the whole purpose for the right-hand man is to tell the producer, "No." - So as quickly as 'Hello,' Richard hands the right-hand man his knit coat to put up on the hanger, knowing the weight and shape of his 45 caliber auto would be unmistakable.

The right-hand man's face froze and he went into halting slow motion performing the duty. The meeting proceeded happily with the producer in perfect love with what he read, spilling over the pages like a smorgasbord of delights. He couldn't believe how much he loved it and how there was such perfect agreement from his man.

It was all so perfect. They signed right there.

The Future

Certainly there's been times I've had my doubts - but after all, it always was my plan to live forever; and if I'm living forever, obviously, I'll win the Lotto at some point - right?

Pitch Conference [Hollywood2]

Winston did many scripts, worked on scripts and also did "Foleys", movie sound effects. This is a room of brickabrac and garden utensils. Strange wooden devices and reed bundles. All to make the odd sounds that every audience has heard in the background of every movie sound-track.

Winston's pitch conference:

He arrives at the curb about 1:00 in the afternoon. The picture window on the third floor jarringly rattles. Someone's back and flailing arms are pressed against the glass by an unseen attacker.

Dropping his eyes to the entrance, he proceeds in. The third floor office is a bare room with two chairs; and the picture window. The producer barges in sporting a three week growth, dirty beach pants and tennies with no laces. Half his face is obscured behind a blanket of thick cigarette smoke.

The guy rattles a few comments when he grabs the script. Winston sits facing him six feet away.

They sit in silence while the producer reads through.

From a Dream

Imagine you're in a dark and foggy world. Gray everywhere. Thin trees jut up and disappear in the low overcast. The ground is purplish and seems to take you with it. You are walking a path. It comes from behind and stretches before you.

If you change direction, you instantly walk a new path. You see the ground is a constant intersection of different paths. They are pushing themselves together from all directions and heading in all directions. They are a fabric. You are the walker but the paths are endless and your feet cannot escape.

Smart Mouth -
Palo Alto Military Academy. 4th grade, 10 years old.

I don't know why they allowed me to take over Parade Command. But I knew I would show them. I would take the platoons out like a Sunday drive. 1st Platoon, Right Face and Forward March. Second platoon Half-right, March. 3rd platoon Forward March, then right. I was going to march 2nd Platoon at angle toward center field and weave 3rd Platoon straight through them to have all three Platoons arrive at the far edge of the field before bringing them forward into the center. A sparkling presentation. I was doing the weave pretty good when laughter called my attention to 1st Platoon, grinding into the far fence. I was relieved of duty.

Top Session
We're at my house in Bolinas. John Grunfest is there, Armando is there, Steven Josel is there, that piano player who was in Downbeat, the guy who later cut his arm in half helping a friend move a piece of glass, he was there. A couple of others were there and it is a full out Free Jazz Jam session in the afternoon. One guy was blowing a simple little plastic Recorder. He'd cut through with some searing, stabbing lines which the whole band would blast and soar around. The whole thing was free jazz, so it was all over the place.
Finally the day wound down and the session broke off. People talking music, packing up and then slowly leaving out. Only Tui and this guy, who was her new boyfriend, stayed around and we all talked. I asked him what he played, certainly not a plastic recorder. Flute and sax? He said he didn't play, he found it on the table, just blew as hard as he could and wiggled his hands over the holes.

Nyquil

I got the crud bad. Relief is pursued from the dwindling resources at the little mountain store.

Vicks Nyquil is green. 3 table-spoons deliver the dose via a supplied cup. Miserable consecutive days have me purchase all four bottles. On the weekend, I hit the store and buy the one remaining "Vicks Cold and Flu" which is red but has the same proportions as the green, 3 to 1. It's Sunday, the crud is unrelenting, I've used all the green and take my regular dose but now of the red. Nothing happens. If fact, if anything, I only feel a windy sensation. I pick up the red and see the same, expected proportions, 3 to 1 - it's difficult however because the ink on the label seems smeared away from the print making it hard to read. I hand it to my live-in who says yes, it's 3 to 1. She has a hard time with the little print as well - "3 teaspoons."

I say: "Table spoons, Tbs, table spoons, yes?" She says "No... -tsp" - I say "b - table spoons - right?" No, "it's a p - tsp - teaspoons." I have taken over ten times the correct dosage. My heart is racing. Things are strange.

She phones the clinic, who phones the CDC. They say, "Oh, he's gonna die."

If you take too much Dextromethorphan, your heart explodes. They say they'll send a helicopter. I'm laying down listening to voices and people scurrying about. Eventually, they sent a couple nurses to sit with me at home. They held my hand and I watched them - they seemed at the bank of a stream and I was just under the surface, holding their hand.

The Most Desired Woman in the World
An internet contest to establish the "Most Desired Woman in the World" turned when someone suggested, "Obviously, the most desired woman must be the woman who is desired by the most people"
Where upon simple addition found that the most Desired Woman in the World must be: Progressive Insurance's - FLO.

Jihad
A large, disgruntled man in Cairo complained about America. He said that while they admire many aspects of our National character, "you are a deviant, morally debased society that spreads perversion, evil and decadence throughout the world"
Well, how do we do that?
"America disrupts families and are a threat to religion and social order"
But you said you admire our character.
"Yes, but other stuff - you do to us"
What stuff?
(pause)
- What stuff - What do we do? What are you talking about?
(pause) - "It's illegal."
What is illegal?
"It's illegal to watch"
What is?
"Baywatch"
Baywatch!?
"Yes, (sweeping gesture to the street, where hundreds of TV Dishes hang from every building and roof-top)
- it is sinful and comes into every home"
Do you watch Baywatch?
"Of course. - And we will have our revenge upon you"

Flash

Dick is being driven home by his friend after an evening at the Casino. They ride through a camera-equipped intersection when the automatic flash snaps. As they ride away, his friend gets visibly upset. He's sure he was in the green. He begins a tirade about how morally corrupt it is to fleece the unsuspecting with these speed-traps. They should be illegal. These two-bit towns should be sued. He gets so worked up, he turns the car around and loops back. When they drive up, the thing flashes again! Now he goes off like a Roman Candle. The cameras are a violation of our Constitutional Rights. He reels the car back around and slows to observe. Waiting long enough to be sure the light is GREEN when he crosses. - It gets him again. -

He gets all three in the mail. Naturally, he demanded Dick be his witness in court. He slammed all three disputed tickets down and read the court, the riot act including his poorly rendered notions about the Founders of America and Rights bequeathed us from English Common Law and how he wasn't speeding and didn't run that non-Red non-Stop Light.

The Judge agreed but pointed out to him the tickets were for not wearing his seat-belt, which could be clearly seen in all three photos submitted. $300/per = $900. Pay the Clerk.

Smoke

Rosalie was three with curly hair and Peter, four. They were strapped in and cozy when their plane went down in the Solomons. Natives found them and brought them to their jungle village where the witch doctor had his hut. He came out looking down; they looked up with their big eyes. He brought them in to the fire past a string of shrunken heads. They looked up at the heads and Peter asked, "How do you do that?"

The Witch Doctor leaned down on his haunches, his white eyes glistening in the fire-light, "...First - you cut the head off and then cut up the back to the top of the scalp -"

Peter and Rosalie looked wide-eyed.

"Then you cut and pull the flesh away from the skull, folding it down over the face; cutting it from the bone until the the whole thing just falls into your hand."

The Witch Doctor's eyes glance back and forth.

Peter and Rosalie are disturbed and look to each other before the Witch Doctor continues, "Then you sew up the back of the head and sew the mouth shut so it can't tell anyone. Sort of a hear no evil, speak no evil, kind-of a thing."

The children have never heard of this so the Witch Doctor adds, "Then you hang it by the hair and SMOKE it."

Peter queries, "Smoke it?"

"Yeah, like smoked salmon. -To preserve it. Kind of a locks 'n Bagels kind a thing."

The kids look at him. He looks back, "It shrinks up and turns black."

Peter and Rosalie look at each other and then back up to the Witch Doctor, who replied,

"Well, you asked."

Holding the World Up

Robert Cole

Also Available from Falcons Press

The Falcons of Gebtu

The Falcons of Gebtu
Magical Journey to the
Real Warrior Queen of Egypt

Adults over 13

Children's Section

Sollie

Little Lefty Finds Her Way

Squirrels
Going
Nuts

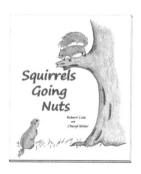

Please visit

Falcons Press ⬦ com
≈ Publishers of Wonderful Things

info@falconspress.com